Resilience
Education

Resilience
Education

JOEL H. BROWN
MARIANNE D'EMIDIO-CASTON
BONNIE BENARD

CORWIN PRESS, INC.
A Sage Publications Company
2455 Teller Road
Thousand Oaks, CA 91320-2218
E-mail: order@corwinpress.com
Call: 805-499-9774 Fax: 800-4-1-SCHOOL
www.corwinpress.com

For information:

 Corwin Press, Inc.
A Sage Publications Company
2455 Teller Road
Thousand Oaks, California 91320
E-mail: order@corwinpress.com

Sage Publications Ltd.
6 Bonhill Street
London EC2A 4PU
United Kingdom

Sage Publications India Pvt. Ltd.
M-32 Market
Greater Kailash I
New Delhi 110 048 India

Printed in the United States of America

Library of Congress Cataloging-in-Publication Data

Brown, Joel H.
    Resilience education / by Joel H. Brown, Marianne D'Emidio-Caston, and Bonnie Benard.
    p. cm.
        Includes bibliographical references (p. 95) and index.
    ISBN 0-7619-7817-8 (cloth: acid free paper)
    ISBN 0-7619-7626-4 (pbk.: acid free paper)
    1. Socially handicapped children—Education—United States. 2. Multicultural education—United States. 3. Resilience (Personality trait) in children. I. D'Emido-Caston, Marianne. II. Benard, Bonnie. III. Title.
    LC4091 .B758 2000
    371.826'94—dc21

                                                          00-009565

01   02   03   04   05   06   10   9   8   7   6   5   4   3   2   1

Corwin Editorial Assistant: Catherine Kantor
Production Editor: Denise Santoyo
Editorial Assistant: Candice Crosetti
Typesetter/Designer: Rebecca Evans

Contents

Preface

What would you say if we told you that about 70% of youth who live in the worst of life's conditions learn to thrive by overcoming many of their fiercest challenges? Moreover, ethnicity, social class, and geographic location do not appear to impede their thriving. By studying what has helped these young people overcome adversity, researchers have identified the significant factors contributing to their amazing resilience. This book, written by educators and researchers together, presents a set of principles and practical applications derived from these factors to help educators who work with youth make a difference in their lives.

A plethora of educational jargon describes the condition of thriving in the face of adversity. Health educators discuss *wellness*; community-based youth workers talk about *youth development*; special educators use the term *assets*; and social workers address a *strengths perspective*. Early childhood educators and social psychologists discuss *child and human development*. Those closely involved in alcohol and substance abuse prevention present *protective factor* research. A cross-discipline, integrated look at nearly 40 years of research tells us that identifying and nurturing an individual's capacities rather than focusing on his or her deficits creates a capable, productive, and compassionate person. Resilience education is the process of supporting young people's acquisition of knowledge as well as a lifelong process for learning.

Resilience education signals an advance in how we educate. It represents a paradigmatic shift from transmission education, with an often-unspoken deficit view of young people, toward a developmental approach focused on their strengths. Taking a resilience approach means meeting a young person's needs for belonging, respect, autonomy, and mastery of relevant and meaningful knowledge. It emphasizes well-being by acknowledging competencies and building upon unique talents, interests, and goals. Resilience education uses learners' strengths as entry points to achievement of required curriculum standards.

Taking a Resilience Approach

Taking a resilience approach requires acknowledging and balancing the ongoing tension between short- and long-term goals for learning. When young people learn to utilize their interests and abilities, they engage in an ever-deeper and more complex learning process, which serves them for a lifetime. Fostering resilience prepares young people to work on weaker areas of their development while supporting a positive sense of self.

The research on resilience tells us more than how to educate young people. It also tells us something about the adults who facilitate resilience. From stories of resilience, we find a variety of role relationships describing the adult caregiver and the young person. We find numerous examples of a mentor, support provider, friend, teacher, counselor, neighbor, parent, grandparent, or other relative who plays this vital role in a young person's life. Here is a brief story describing a resilience experience. It comes from one of our former student teachers. This is "Alicia's" story:

> Growing up and going through the U.S. educational system was very painful for me. This is because I came from Mexico when I was eight years old and I was placed three grades lower than where I should have been. My parents could have changed this placement, but they were not aware of how the U.S. educational system worked even to an extent that a child my age should be in fourth grade. I was three years older than all my classmates and I felt very uncomfortable and dumb. I also did not have friends in school because there were not a lot of children who spoke Spanish and I could not speak with the children who spoke English. Every day during recess I used to just stand by the corner of the handball court and cry, hiding from the adults monitoring recess so they could not see me. I would go home wanting to tell my parents, but when I saw them coming home so late after having worked in the fields all day, I decided I would not tell them. I did not want them to feel pain knowing that I was struggling in school. They already had enough to worry about having nine children to support. I also did not want to tell anyone what I was going through. However, I felt terribly angry deep inside because the teachers were not doing enough to help me. I felt even more frustrated when the teachers would have me sit (often) alone in the back of the classroom to do a crossword puzzle instead of participating in the regular class lessons and activities. I

felt very humiliated to be singled out as inferior. Some children would even laugh at me and the teacher did not notice because she habitually ignored me. Since all this was happening, I was so frustrated that I hated school. However, I thought to myself, "But I am going to learn English and prove to all of you that *I can make it.*" Therefore, I went through my first five school years in the U.S. feeling totally frustrated. Finally in sixth grade, I had a teacher who changed my future.

Mrs. Miranda Diaz was the teacher that made this difference. I remember that the first day I met her she smiled at me. No one outside my family had really smiled at me since I left Mexico. After school that first day of class, she came very close to my desk and said to me "hasta mañana" [See you tomorrow]. Every day she talked to me on a one-to-one basis and asked me how I was doing. She also reminded me of going to breakfast in the mornings. She always gave me specific positive feedback on my work such as "You did a great job in spelling, you got 100%" or "I like your drawing because you drew your family." She would tell me that I was smart and that she was sure that I was going to be successful. I told her that when I grow up I wanted to be a teacher like her and her words were "I am sure you will be, and I know you are going to be a great one."

Alicia is a teacher now, making a difference in her own students' lives. Regardless of what kind of official role the adult plays in the child's life, stories like these all have the special trust of a mentoring relationship in common. They show that resilience is fostered when consistent care is given to support the young person. We could use any one of the official roles to describe the mentoring relationship. In this book, we will use the term *educator* to describe the role of the mentor in resilience education.

Resilience educators gain the trust of young people, hold high expectations for achievement, and offer caring support coupled with accountability. They know how to help young people become aware of their own strengths and interests. They hold an ethic of care grounded in authentic relationship. The process of nurturing resilience in a young person also enhances the development of the mentor. It is a mutual learning relationship that is beneficial to both educator and youth. Based on research and many years of experience, we now can say with confidence that relationships are *the* medium for nurturing human beings that thrive.

WHAT RESLIENCE EDUCATION IS

Thriving in the face of adversity through mutually beneficial relationships goes beyond clichés about empowerment. Resilience education provides specific means to empower. In resilience education, the educator is part of a reciprocal cycle in which he or she is energized to take reasonable risks with creativity and to support his or her own as well as young people's dreams, goals, and aspirations. At the same time, students are empowered to experiment with decisions about their interests and strengths in the context of a learning environment in which they will be supported, not penalized. Moreover, students are given opportunities to contribute their gifts through service to others in their classroom, school, and community. In specific ways then, resilience education signifies humane empowerment.

To this point, we have been speaking of resilience and the significant factors that help the young person overcome adversity. The 70% of these youth who "make it" are finding the support they need. With the help of educators who learn the principles of resilience education, the 30% of students who are currently "falling through the cracks," "dropping out," becoming burdens on an already burgeoning criminal justice system, or otherwise not contributing to the common good of the society can be helped as well. This book helps you address these young people's needs. A goal of this book is to help you as an educator make a difference in the lives of the students who might otherwise fall through the cracks.

We make the additional argument that the resilience education approach also applies to normally developing, already motivated youth. State by state we are engaged in a national setting of educational standards. We recognize as a society that schools must do better for *all* our students. The focus for educational reform has been comprehensive, with calls for an overhaul of curriculum, reading instruction, math instruction, governance, family-school relationships, inclusion of special education students, and so forth. We are challenged by the responsibility to meet the needs of all learners in the new millennium. Reform efforts must be mindful that fast-paced global change will be part of the future. In such a social milieu, the resilience of each student needs to be developed. To find paths for themselves in the global society, all young people, of all diverse cultures, languages, and economic backgrounds, need to develop their capacities to meet challenges with problem-solving attitudes. They all need to find and nurture relationships, see possibilities and potentials, and use their imaginations. These skills must then be translated into collaborating with others across the boundaries of diversity, a hallmark of the global society. Our approach to resilience is a general one focused on building a climate and a process within that climate that works to benefit all, including the educator.

What does "building a climate and a process within that climate that works to benefit all, including the educator" mean? Although several elements will be described throughout the book, let's look at one specific example, the importance of affect in the classroom. In traditional educational approaches, students' needs have often been addressed piecemeal, focusing primarily on their academic achievement. Attention to students' social, emotional, or ethical—their affective—development is regularly left to the implicit curriculum. Little attention has been paid to the links between students' strengths and abilities, their academic success, and the construction of identity. Even less attention has been paid to the role teachers or other educators play in strengthening those links. The focus on academic achievement almost totally ignores the role of emotion or relationships in the educational process. Many teachers in the field today received no training in the affective side of learning. This suggests that the teacher's skill of building authentic relationships and supporting their students' capabilities is innate, that it depends on charisma and natural interpersonal skills. Students' affective development and capacities for resilience are left to teachers who believe that these dimensions of human development are fundamental to learning. These teachers have found through trial, error, and perseverance how to utilize affect in learning. We now know that affect is an essential ingredient in learning and acquiring a lifelong process for learning. Paying attention to how children feel about learning or their participation provides opportunities for the teachable moment. The resulting connection between educator and young people can lead to deep learning. Yet few have generated a set of principles for developing resilience using affect in education. It follows then that rarely have such principles been systemically applied in public school classrooms.

We honor and acknowledge that there are many teachers and people who work with youth who *are* advocates for students. Indeed, it is their efforts that have contributed to the success of the 70% who do thrive. By making explicit what resilience educators do, this book will help any person in any environment working with young people to learn how to emphasize the resilience that exists within each of us. We like to say that resilience education is not identifying which people are resilient, but rather, identifying what resilience exists in each person.

Resilience Education and This Book

In resilience education, the focus is on the development of young people's interests and strengths and the development of their identity. This does not ignore the use of "extrinsic motivation" with some children at certain times. Instead, our concept of resilience education simply says that when a young person's motivation is intrinsic, he or she is likely to learn more deeply and to go on to acquire a lifelong learning process. Rather than focusing primarily on addressing a young person's problems, which often results in labeling the youth as being "at risk" for this, that, or the other thing, we work in a completely different way. In resilience education, we emphasize caring youth-adult relationships, high expectation messages, and opportunities for young people to be actively engaged in their learning. Through fostering personal awareness, responsibility, and decision-making capabilities and through focusing on each person's healthy overall development, we help young people to see possibilities and potentials in their lives and to reduce each young person's risk for poor development. The transition from identification and isolation of individual deficits toward promoting the person's awareness of potential is a fundamental shift in education. How any educator in any learning situation can facilitate learning and development through resilience education is the focus of this book.

In the following chapters, we show how resilience education evolves from theory to principles to practice. We hope that as you understand the assumptions guiding the principles and creatively apply them to your work with young people, the experience will be dynamic for you as well as your students. At the same time, as you help your students acquire personal knowledge and deepen their learning by building on their interests and strengths, your role as educator will transform as well. As the responsibility of being an active learner is taken up by the students, you will come to trust that young people can be increasingly responsible for their own learning.

Once resilience educational principles are learned, they will become second nature. The practices discussed in this book will help young people identify their own interests, build upon their own strengths, and engender their own lifelong learning processes. Chapters identifying specific principles of resilience education follow a history of resilience. Experiential examples asking you, the reader, to participate are provided throughout the book. They are intended to build on one another throughout the book as your skills do.

Although this book discusses the process of delivering resilience education, it is important to note what we leave up to your own professional discretion. How you decide to apply resilience education in your classroom is up to you. Before jumping full force into experiential exercises or other participatory activities, resilience educators consider a number of things. Variables such as the developmental levels of your students or the values of your community serve as just two examples. In this book, we do not explicitly address each of these variables. Instead, we develop an orientation toward working with them. As you enhance your skills to develop resilience in young people and to build resilience education into your practice, you will come to reflect on how to more carefully consider the specific variables that emerge. This book is designed with a fundamental trust in the professional discretion of each educator.

ACKNOWLEDGMENTS

The contributions of the following reviewers are gratefully acknowledged:

Paul Englesberg
Woodring College of Education
Western Washington University, Bellingham, Washington

Judith Olson
Instructional Services Consultant
Lakeland Area Education Agency 3, Cylinder, Iowa

Mary Ann Sweet
School Counselor
Tomball Elementary, Tomball, Texas

Raymond Francis
Professor
Central Michigan University, Alma, Michigan

Judith Randi, Ed.D.
Professor of Education
Columbia University, New York, New York

Patrick Akos
Counselor and Educator
University of Virginia, Charlottesville, Virginia

About the Authors

Joel H. Brown, PhD, MSW, is Executive Director of the Center for Educational Research and Development (CERD; *www.cerd.org*), a Berkeley-based nonprofit evaluation, research, and policy development organization committed to the development of resilience-based policies and programs. He is an educational researcher who has been at the forefront of making evident in people's lives the relevance of youth development-oriented educational research, evaluation, and practice, and his clients have included many local, state, and federal agencies. He has published numerous books and articles on these topics, including the nationally renowned "In Their Own Voices: Students and Educators Evaluate California School-Based Drug Alcohol and Tobacco Education (DATE) Programs." Commissioned by the California State Department of Education, this remains the only study of its kind to involve extensive interviews and surveys of children, adolescents, community members, teachers, principals, and superintendents. His work includes editorship and coeditorship of a book series devoted to the dynamics of planned change in education. The first two books in this series, *Integrating Consciousness for Human Change* (1996) and *The Multicultural Dynamics of Educational Change* (2000) are currently available. Brown's research and commentary has been noted and solicited in myriad media outlets, such as the *New York Times, Boston Globe, Los Angeles Times,* and National Public Radio (NPR). Before earning his doctorate in Education at the University of California, Santa Barbara, Brown earned an MSW from the University of California, Berkeley.

Marianne D'Emidio-Caston, PhD, is a recognized leader in the research, evaluation, and development of educational process. She has more than 25 years of field experience as an educator, administrator, and researcher, and her background in teaching and learning theory, school administration, and school change lends a broad perspective to her work. Among numerous scholarly publications, her coauthored article "Making Meaning in

Classrooms: An Investigation of Cognitive Processes in Aspiring Teachers, Experienced Teachers, and Their Peers," published in *American Educational Research Journal*, received the Association of Teacher Educators' Distinguished Research in Teacher Education Award in 1995. Her chapter "Preparing Teachers to Serve Children and Families with Diverse Backgrounds" was recently published in *Joining Hands: Preparing Teachers to Make Meaningful Home-School Connections*, issued by the California Department of Education and the California Commission on Teacher Credentialing. She holds an MA in Educational Policy and Administration and a PhD in Confluent Education from UC Santa Barbara.

Bonnie Benard, MA, is Senior Program Associate with WestEd (formerly Far West Laboratory for Educational Research and Development) and also works with the Center for Educational Research and Development. She is a nationally renowned figure in the field of prevention theory, policy, and practice, most recently earning recognition for introducing and conceptualizing resiliency theory and application. In 1992 she received the Award of Excellence in Prevention from the National Association of State Alcohol and Drug Abuse Directors and the National Prevention Network, in 1995 she received the Paul Templin Award for Service from the Western Regional Center for Safe and Drug-Free Schools and Communities, and in 1997 she received the Spirit of Crazy Horse Award for her advocacy of resilience-based practice.

To hear; to understand (T'ing)

The Chinese word for understanding is made up of six parts:
ear, precious, perfect, vessel, unity, and heart.

To understand means to hear with your heart.

Crisis as opportunity (wéi jī)

The Chinese word for crisis is made up of two parts:
danger and opportunity.

Danger—originally pictured as a man on the edge of a precipice

Opportunity—a reminder of the seemingly small but important
opportunity that can come out of danger

To George and Judith Brown,
our teachers, our students.

I

SUPPORTING EVIDENCE
FOR RESILIENCE

HERE IS THE BEGINNING of our educational adventure, where the choices of how to proceed in this book are yours. We want to make explicit our understanding that choices exist, even when we read books. Developing choices can also become part of how you work with students. Making choices available provides us with more resilience-developing options. So at several junctures throughout the book we will note choices that you might make. By doing this we are modeling a resilience education adventure.

The following three chapters contain the research you need to support development of resilience education. Please feel free to read them in depth, leaf through them, or skip to the last section of Chapter 3, beginning on page 28, where resilience education is described and defined. Then proceed with Part II, where the PORT-able approach to resilience education is developed in detail. Enjoy the beginning of your journey!

The Limitations of
a Risk Orientation

RESILIENCE HAS BECOME A POWERFUL WAY of thinking about how to work with young people in schools, challenging the historically familiar approach called the "risk orientation."

RISK FACTORS AND THE MEDICAL MODEL

The risk orientation begins with the application of a medical model to education. For many years the medical field has known that chronic high cholesterol is a major cause of heart disease. In the medical vernacular, chronic high cholesterol is known as a "risk factor" for heart disease. The medical thinking is that if those with high cholesterol can be identified early, then doctors can take action or influence patients to act on their own behalf to treat or prevent their heart disease. With proper intervention, such as having the patient change his or her diet, exercise, and take prescription medicine, the risk factor of high cholesterol can be minimized or removed, with the direct effect of reducing the risk for heart disease.

Why is the concept of the risk factor so important to this book? For nearly 20 years now, the medical concept of a risk factor has been applied to education. Researchers looked hard at which life factors contributed to young people's failures to respond to given educational expectations. As risk factors were identified, educational policies and programs were developed using the specific risk factors, as if they, like cholesterol, were direct causes of a child's inability to meet educational expectations. Educators of every sort now use measures of risk as a means to try to predict failure of all sorts. Many now have a "risk orientation" toward young people, a belief that they are generally subject to failure. In effect, we have become a nation at risk. Let's examine how this occurred.

A NATION AT RISK?

Both the National Commission on Excellence in Education (in 1983) and the Education Commission of the States (in 1988) used the term *at risk* to describe a culturally and economically disadvantaged society. These reports suggested that the conditions in which children lived outside of school had a greater impact on their success in school than the school itself.

The policy and program recommendations from the National Commission on Excellence in Education and from the Education Commission of the States prompted researchers to more specifically address risk factors and clusters of risk factors correlated with school failure. For example, based on certain "risk" characteristics, such as divorce, children were believed to have increased risk of accidents, delinquency, and drug abuse (Bell & Bell, 1993; Coie et al., 1993; Gillmore et al., 1991; Hawkins, Catalano, & Miller, 1992; Hawkins, Lishner, Jenson, & Catalano, 1987; Rossi, 1994). In 1995, Brown and D'Emidio-Caston summarized various and wide-ranging risk factors claimed by other researchers:

> Risk factors include contextual, interpersonal, and individual dimensions. Contextual factors include (but are not limited to) local laws and norms favorable toward substance using behavior, such as the availability of alcohol at gas stations or quick stop markets. Interpersonal and individual substance abuse risk factors include (but are not limited to) a low commitment to school as well as academic failure. According to the "risk factor model," if students have a low degree of commitment to school and/or are academically failing, they are more likely to become substance abusers than other students not possessing these characteristics (Hawkins et al., 1992). Furthermore, it is believed that risk factors are cumulative; a

student with more risk factors is more likely to become a substance abuser (Newcomb & Bentler, 1988). (Brown & D'Emidio-Caston, 1995, pp. 452-453)

The research has moved into policy. Brown and Horowitz (1993) found that, when describing program funding requirements, the California State Department of Education identified at least 36 factors from the research literature that were linked to the inability of young people to develop in a healthy way. To gain funding, school districts had to show how they responded to specific risk factors. These funding guidelines allowed people to transfer the risk orientation back onto schools (California State Department of Education, 1991-1992).

Across the country, services aimed specifically at "at-risk" and "high-risk" youth were funded under such government programs as Title 1 of the Elementary and Secondary Education Act and the Drug Free Schools and Communities Act of 1986 (Office of Substance Abuse Prevention, 1989). Risk factors continue to guide funding in specific educational areas; special education, English as a second language, violence prevention, and drug abuse are just a few. After nearly 20 years, risk factors dominate the thinking about students who may not be successful in the educational system. Proactive programs are oriented toward serving at-risk students to prevent their failure in school. To make them eligible for those programs, young people are labeled "at risk," often long before they actually demonstrate failure.

RESULTS OF THE RISK ORIENTATION: A DEFICIT VIEW OF YOUNG PEOPLE IN SCHOOL

Given the widespread use of the risk orientation to determine funding and available resources to help students at risk, it is reasonable to expect that key academic and health and safety indices would show improvement. However, we are challenged to find such significant gains in either academic or health and safety data. Instead, in the late 1980s and throughout the 1990s, students' achievement in the United States, even that of our most advanced students, was poor in comparison to students in other countries. For example, the United States "was among the lowest performing

countries on both the mathematics and science general knowledge assessments." (Forgione, 1998). Furthermore, across the country, young people's
drug use nearly doubled by 1993 from its low point in the mid-1980s
(Johnston, O'Malley, & Bachman, 1999). The apparent disparity in the
achievement of whole groups of students (e.g., African American and
Latino students, particularly in low-income areas) and the anomaly of
high-achieving schools with similar populations (e.g., Debra Meier's Central Park East in New York City, the 90-90-90 Schools in Milwaukee) led researchers to this question: Which factors were truly significant predictors
of school failure?

With findings like these, researchers began to question the risk orientation's effectiveness (Baizerman & Compton, 1992; Blue-Swadener &
Lubeck, 1995; Brown & D'Emidio-Caston, 1995; Brown & Horowitz, 1993;
Fine, 1993; Placier, 1993; Richardson, 1990). Which so-called risk factors actually caused school failure, and which were merely correlated with school
failure? For example, did drug use cause school failure, or did school failure
cause drug use? If the factors were so wide ranging and so many young people were consequently considered to be at risk, then of what utility was the
model? Going back to our earlier medical example, unlike the chronic presence of high cholesterol in the blood, which predicts heart disease, risk factors seemed to be related to problems but were not clearly or consistently
shown to predict long-term problems for young people. The lack of predictable outcomes in the risk factor model became an inherent problem in the
research itself.

Because of the multitude of risk factors, many educators came to view
virtually every child as being at risk for some kind of failure. Teachers began
to describe their students' lack of success as related to specific "risk" factors
such as not doing homework, habitually coming late to school, having fre-
quent absences, or having little or no parental contact with the school.
Look at how one school official viewed students in his school: "We are addressing the risk factors that show up, with the idea that it's real hard for me
to point out which of our kids are not at risk" (Brown & D'Emidio-Caston,
1995, p. 468). Some risk factors seemed more powerful than others in predicting a student's success or failure. A child's inability to read by third
grade, for example, prompts an enormous effort to remedy this risk in
young learners. Nevertheless, researchers wondered, in the context of normal adolescent development, which young people were not subject to typical risk factors such as "alienation" or "rebelliousness"? By the mid-1990s,
findings were reported describing the stigma of labeling young people as

having something wrong with them before they had demonstrated failure. The implementation of the model itself had become a way of labeling young people as being at risk for a multitude of negative outcomes with or without just cause. In 1992, Baizerman and Compton summarized the problems of the risk orientation by noting,

> In many schools, this process results in the majority of students being identified as at-risk. This is hardly surprising, since the educational use of the term at-risk does not meet the test of the public health definition—that is, it is not known whether the characteristics used for identification actually predict which students are most likely to drop out of school . . . the whole field of education used the concept of risk as part of an ideology, thereby joining science, mathematics, and morality. (pp. 8-9)

Baizerman and Compton (1992) continued their criticism with the observation that the application of the risk factor model creates a socioeducational population of at-risk students and suggests that the students are both the problem and its cause. As a consequence of this negative view of young people, the school is absolved of blame for failures to successfully educate each young person. Throughout the 1990s researchers became bolder with their criticisms. Authors such as Blue-Swadener and Lubeck (1995) asked "whether the term 'at risk' is ever justified or serves children and families" (p. xi).

There are several conclusions that can be drawn about the risk factor model. First, there are so many risk factors correlated with school failure that it has been impossible for educators to use the model in schools. For many in the educational community, there was a logical confusion when correlated factors discovered in risk factor research were misinterpreted as causing educational failure. Second, funding based on one or another risk factor effectively tied the hands of program developers to remedy the adversity youth face in any comprehensive way. Third, risk-based education and policies maintain a historical way of viewing young people as inherently deviant, labeling them, and maintaining their marginality in the school community. Finally, taking a risk orientation focuses the center of the problem on the student or the student's family, not on the school or pedagogy, which have such a great deal to do with the student's navigation through adversity.

MAINTAINING THE RISK ORIENTATION

Despite the spreading understanding that the model was for the most part a failure, policymakers attempted to bolster its application with additional recommendations. For example, the U.S. Department of Education provided this school district funding opportunity:

> Under the authority of the Safe and Drug-Free Schools and Communities Act, a competition will be conducted to create effective model projects to provide alternatives to expulsion, i.e. meaningful alternative forms of schooling outside the classrooms for children expelled or suspended from school. . . .
> With the growing numbers of "at-risk" youth and the increased efforts of schools to reduce violence and maintain order, we anticipate that the number of children removed from regular classroom settings may increase significantly. This competition will serve to meet our responsibility to continue to provide a meaningful education for those troubled youngsters. (Modzeleski, 1995)

Without questioning the basic assumption of the risk orientation, more resources could now be devoted to providing services that were designed under the risk factor thesis. Perhaps because it replaces "tension and uncertainty with a measure of clarity, meaning, confidence, and security" (Edelman, 1964, p. 61), the risk orientation became a powerful educational frame of reference.

THE RISK ORIENTATION DOES NOT MEET SCIENTIFIC RIGOR OR TODAY'S EDUCATIONAL NEEDS

The failures of the risk factor model are more than the failures to specifically identify and help young people who are most vulnerable. The failures are more than the educational implications of taking a deficit view of young people. The most important failures of the risk factor model are those that result from a narrow view of modern education. Today's education demands that all young people learn to be resilient in the face of challenging conditions. All youngsters must have the capacity to avoid problem behavior, but to thrive in a global economy young people must do more than that. They must also acquire basic knowledge and skills and develop a lifelong learning process, so that each may continually respond to today's fast-paced, changing world.

The increasing recognition of these failures has caused researchers and the educational community to seek an alternative approach that is more than just another program shift built on the same risk orientation model. Resilience is truly an alternative approach constructed from the research on how children facing adversity succeed and on what can be done to support them as they face the struggles in their lives.

2

Understanding the Human Capacity for Healthy Adaptation

THIS CHAPTER TELLS THE STORY of how our understanding of resilience has resulted from an often serendipitous research odyssey.

THE HISTORICAL EMERGENCE OF RESILIENCE

In their classic book *The Invulnerable Child,* Anthony and Cohler (1987) described a social historical overview of risk, vulnerability, and resilience. In the first chapter, Anthony and Cohler retold the plot of Albert Camus's (1942) "The Stranger." Camus described the life and private thoughts of Mersault, his leading character, who spent a great deal of his life in prison. Mersault's existence was marked with major changes in his life situation, often measured by various kinds of deprivation. Though his affect flattened under the most difficult circumstances, Mersault dealt with even the most extreme conditions of prison with impressive adaptability. By psychologically detaching from the immediate situation, he was "happy" and invulnerable to adversity. Camus's depiction of Mersault and Anthony and Cohler's description of the "invulnerable child" illustrate one of the most important social science discoveries of this century—the human capacity for healthy adaptation even in the face of risk and adversity.

In 1972, after a 20-year research period, Hinkle found that people experienced patterned susceptibilities to illness. Those who had experienced previous vulnerabilities to disease displayed life patterns of illness. Conversely, those who were not seen as previously vulnerable did not display significant illness patterns. The power of Hinkle's study was the serendipitous finding that some people who experienced difficulties similar to those of others did not display a pattern of life illness as expected (Hinkle, 1974). In these individuals, the processes of handling life's challenges seemed unique:

> The healthiest members of our samples often showed little psychological reaction to events and situations which caused profound reaction in other members of the group . . . the frustration of apparent important desires, or the failure to obtain apparently important goals produced no profound or long lasting reaction. (p. 40)

Hinkle's (1974) finding of certain "invulnerable" individuals is in curious "sync" with Anthony and Cohler's (1987) work and Camus's (1942) description of Mersault. Based on this early research, Hinkle arrived at five descriptive typologies of people whom he called "invulnerables":

> First, there is the "invulnerable" who has a "sociopathic," uninvolved approach to the world and is strategically estranged from it.
>
> There is also the "invulnerable" who leads a charmed life because of the over protectiveness of the mother . . . because he [she] is left unchallenged by the actualities of life.
>
> Another group of "invulnerables" [who thrived despite adversity] turned out to be accident-prone from the endless risks that they take, especially when an audience is around.
>
> The true "invulnerables" are also true heroes who tend to leave the scene of heroism. Instead of breaking down when the going gets rough, they perform better than ever. These invulnerables display a high degree of competence in spite of (or sometimes because of) stressful environments and experiences.
>
> A special subgroup of "invulnerables" comprises those who have bounced back and continue to rebound from high risks to vulnerability. Their creative activity relieves their overwhelming sense of vulnerability, but as it abates, they become susceptible to breakdown. It is a lifelong struggle by often very miserable people, but society benefits from it. (pp. 42-45)

This early research appeared to show that there are "types" of naturally invulnerable people. Later research would show that resilience is not *only* available to a select few—most people can be resilient. Later resilience research would show that the environmental factor of human support for others is what most often helps to facilitate resilience. Even when considering the later research, which completely altered earlier concepts of resilience, it is important to note the early contributions of researchers such as Hinkle (1974), who brought embryonic concepts of resilience to our attention.

THRIVING IN THE FACE OF ADVERSITY: RESILIENCE AND THE WHOLE CHILD

Several researchers moved from exploring the phenomenon of invulnerability to how these "invulnerables" develop and thrive (Heider, 1966; Moriarty, 1961; Murphy, 1956, 1962; Murphy & Moriarty, 1976). Their primary contributions were twofold: First, they focused on the importance of coping—the "how" of resilience. Second, they linked resilience to the context of the whole child. In 1987, Moriarty concluded:

> Resilience as I have conceived of it, in terms of recovery over a shorter or long time, involves global aspects of the whole child—growth and growth drive.... Resilience, like competence and adaptation as outcomes of coping, is an evaluative concept, not a unitary trait. The resilient child is oriented toward the future, is living ahead, with hope. (p. 101)

With this work, the resilience approach was linked with life development (e.g., "oriented toward the future") involving a comprehensive view of the whole child (e.g., "global aspects of the whole child—growth and growth drive").

It is important to take a moment to note the convergence of parallel lines of research. Long before resilience researchers focused on the lifetime development of the whole child, progressive educators and developmental psychologists took this focus. Early childhood educators are familiar with the philosophical tradition that centers on the development of the whole child (Bredekamp, 1986; Dewey, 1897, 1899, 1902; Kohlberg & Meyer, 1972; Montessori, 1912; Piaget, 1973; Steiner, 1988). Piaget's studies of how children develop their understanding of mathematics, time, moral judgment, and so forth, and Kohlberg and Meyer's contributions to our understanding of moral development are often cited by educators who hold a holistic, developmental approach to teaching and learning. This historical tradition in education and developmental psychology converges with resilience research to support a holistic view of youth in the context of lifelong development.

RESILIENCE: EACH PERSON'S SELF-RIGHTING MECHANISMS

The concept of development over one's life cycle is supported by a number of important works by people such as Garmezy (1983, 1991), Rutter (1987, 1991), and Werner and Smith (1982). In working with groups of children (32 children with life-threatening congenital heart defects and 29 severely handicapped children), Garmezy (1987) found that, "except for the conduct disordered group of children, only a minority of our at risk children seemed deficit ridden. Thus, presuming that these children were at risk, the absence of disorder in the majority suggested . . . protective factors" (p. 163).

These findings are in accord with two pioneering lines of resilience research, by Rutter and by Werner. Rutter's research focused on institutionalized children. In his seminal work "Psychosocial Resilience and Protective Mechanisms," Rutter (1987) advanced a shift from a focus on invulnerability to resilience and to specific "protective factors" that we see evolving over the lives of these children. Rutter (1979) found that in the face of great adversity, such as poverty, poor housing, and family difficulties, "[n]early half of these children are well-adjusted, one in seven has some kind of outstanding ability, and one in eleven shows above average attainment in mathematics" (p. 49). Rutter (1979) asserted that resilience could be explained by several constructs:

> [When the findings are all in, the explanation will probably include the patterning of stresses, individual differences caused by both constitutional and experiential factors, compensating experiences outside the home, the development of self-esteem, the scope and range of available opportunities, an appropriate degree of environmental structure and control, the availability of personal bonds and intimate relationships, and the acquisition of coping skills. (p. 71)

Rutter's work is important for at least two reasons. First, he was one of the first to call attention to the idea of developing resilience as a useful way of promoting the well-being of all rather than targeting specific deficiencies found in an at-risk population (Rutter, 1979, 1981, 1987). His work has a seemingly simple though significant implication for us: We can be most effective in helping youth by promoting their well-being. Second, he provided new support for specific protective factors that promote resilience in children.

By 1985 Rutter found that protective factors were essential for development. During that period, he moved beyond the mere description of the resilience phenomena, explaining the underlying psychological process by which resilience occurred. Rutter (1985) noted,

1. To begin with, a person's response to any stressor will be influenced by his appraisal of the situation and by his capacity to process the experience, attach meaning to it, and incorporate it into his belief system. . . .

2. It matters greatly how people deal with adversities and life stressors—perhaps not so much in the particular coping strategy employed but in the fact that they do act and not simply react. . . .

3. [P]eople's ability to act positively is a function of their self-esteem and feelings of self-efficacy as much as of their range of problem solving skills. . . .

4. [S]uch a cognitive set seems to be fostered by features as varied as secure stable affectational relationships and success, achievement and positive experiences, as well as by temperamental attributes. . . .

5. [S]uch personal qualities seem to be operative as much in their effects on interactions with and responses from other people, as in their role in regulating individual responses to life events. . . .

6. [C]oping successfully with stress situations can be strengthening: throughout life, it is normal to have to meet challenges and overcome difficulties. The promotion of resilience does not lie in an avoidance of stress, but rather in encountering stress at a time and in a way that allows self-confidence and social competence to increase through mastery and appropriate responsibility. . . .

7. [A]ll the evidence points to the importance of developmental links. Protection does not primarily lie in the buffering effect of

some supportive factor, operating at one point in time, or even over a prolonged time. Rather, the quality of resilience resides in how people deal with life changes and what they do about their situations. (p. 608)

By the mid-1980s, within a small but growing research community, resilience had become a solidly established frame for conceptualizing how people such as educators could work with children facing adversity. The concept of a general self-righting mechanism, available to nearly all people who are provided with sufficient support, was emerging. This is the modern concept of resilience.

RESILIENCE AND PROTECTIVE FACTORS: A LIFELONG HOLISTIC VIEW OF DEVELOPMENT

The many researchers noted previously made essential contributions to the ideas of resilience, but one researcher's dedication stands above the rest. The pioneering work of Emmy Werner and her team of researchers began in 1954 and continues today (Werner, 1986, 1989, 1993; Werner, Bierman, & French, 1971; Werner & Smith, 1977, 1982). In short, Werner's work constitutes not only an important line of resilience research, but one of the most valuable social science studies ever conducted. This research is important for two reasons. First, it provides researchers with key predictive evidence of the relationship between extreme high-risk environments and future psychosocial adaptation. Second, Werner and her colleagues' work explains why those who did not go on to have future coping difficulties were resilient, that is, the factors that predict adolescent success.

In Werner's longitudinal study, pediatricians, public health workers, and psychologists worked together with disadvantaged infants and families from the Hawaiian island of Kauai. Over the years, batteries of diagnostic tests were administered to young people. The researchers used these tests to examine the extent to which they predicted a variety of psychosocial outcomes. At that point, Werner's team made one of its most important observations:

Yet there were others, also vulnerable—exposed to poverty, biological risks, and family instability, and reared by parents with little education or serious mental health problems—who remained invincible and developed into competent and autonomous young adults. (Werner & Smith, 1982, p. 3)

Like Garmezy and Rutter, once such an observation was made, it became both an avenue for research and, even more important, a conceptual approach guiding research. Werner boiled Garmezy's and Rutter's protective factors down to three that helped vulnerable children develop well into adulthood:

1. Dispositional attributes of the individual, such as activity level and sociability, at least average intelligence, competence in communication skills (language, reading), and an internal locus of control

2. Affectational ties within the family that provide emotional support in times of stress, whether from the parent, sibling, spouse, or mate

3. External support systems, whether in school, at work, or church, that reward the individual's competencies and determination and that provide a belief system by which to live (Werner, 1989, p. 80)

In the first factor, Werner notes the importance of certain individual characteristics, which have been enhanced with the proper environment. The second and third characteristics of resilient youth are interconnected. Each involves support: The second involves individual support and the connection of young people with familial and extrafamilial adults, and the third involves the support of a larger community. The supports of others as key parts of developing or facilitating resilience can be summarized by the word *connectedness*. Werner's nearly 40-year research journey shows that being emotionally connected with adults and people in communities is a significant part of what allows nearly 70% of young people in even the worst conditions to thrive despite adversity. It is this general global idea of connectedness that represents both a holistic and positive view of young people and a way to help them develop well over the course of their lifetimes.

Confirmation of Werner's findings is now emerging. New longitudinal research (the National Longitudinal Study of Adolescent Health) has shown that the specific protective factors of "parent-family and perceived school connectedness were protective against every health risk behavior measure except pregnancy" (Resnick et al., 1997, p. 823).

By 1999, many years of research have confirmed the idea that if we promote the well-being of youth, even those in life's worst circumstances can succeed. As Bonnie Benard (1996) summarized:

> In the strictest sense, resiliency research refers to a body of international cross-cultural, life-span developmental studies that followed children born into seriously high risk conditions such as families where parents were mentally ill, alcoholic, abusive or criminal, or in communities that were poverty-stricken or war-torn. The astounding finding from these long-term studies was that at least 50%—and often closer to 70%—of youth growing up in these high-risk conditions did develop social competence despite exposure to severe stress and did overcome the odds to lead successful lives. Furthermore, these studies not only identified the characteristics of these "resilient" youth, several documented the characteristics of the environments—of the families, schools, and communities—that facilitated the manifestation of resilience. (p. 7)

Resilience and protective factor research supports a transactional model of human development (Brofenbrenner, 1979; Piaget, 1929). Research has now established that the nature of the interaction between child or adolescent and caregiver, in the context of a supportive society, is what primarily provides for learning, development, and ultimately resilience (Benard, 1987; Kumpfer, 1990). Relationships are *the* medium for supporting thriving development.

It is essential to note that although risk and resilience are related, developing resilience is not just another aspect of addressing risk. As Brown and Horowitz (1993) noted:

> Protective factors are not merely the opposite of risk factors. Rather, they represent a separate group of factors, defined independently of risk factors. . . . More importantly . . . protective factor researchers do not display the deviance assumption that is found in the risk factor mythology. (pp. 546-547)

What lessons do we draw from resilience research? Because they are so important, we list them here:

- There is long-standing research support for educators who use or want to use a resilience perspective in working with young people.

- Nearly all people, to varying extents, have self-righting mechanisms.

- Resilience research provides strong evidence that successful life outcomes emerge as positive, reliable, and predictable when the focus is on development rather than punishment.

- If those in the worst conditions can survive and thrive, and if the contributing components—such as enriching environment and developing youth-adult connectedness—are mutable, then each young person's learning process can be enriched.

Based on these findings, resilience approaches can be applied to any educational setting, and it is highly likely that benefits will accrue. If we know that nearly 70% of those in the worst conditions can benefit, then it is likely that we can more effectively work with the remaining 30% by making resilience approaches explicit. Finally, others in less adverse conditions should also benefit from the strategies suggested by this pro-youth approach. Thus, taking a resilience approach to education has the potential to meet the needs of a generation certain to face fast-paced global change.

3

Applying a Resilience
Approach to Education

IN EARLIER CHAPTERS we have reviewed the journey from risk to resilience. In this chapter we provide the research support you need to feel confident in delivering the resilience education so important to your own healthy professional development and the healthy development of young people.

One of the strengths of the resilience approach is the multiple lines of research converging at once on the development of the human being as the essence of education. The evidence supporting a resilience approach and its direct application to education is bolstered when we look at learning from the developmental, physiological, educational, and social psychological perspectives. Each of these traditions contributes evidence to support essential assumptions of resilience education. We assert that the evidence is sufficient to guide both principles of action and strategies or interventions necessary to develop resilience in each school, classroom, and young person.

- Decision making: If given proper information, young people can make coherent decisions (developmental psychology).

- Emotion and learning: Feelings directly and indirectly influence learning (physiological and educational psychology, brain science).

- Building on interests and strengths: Intrinsically motivated learning is more meaningful and more deeply connected to the life of the learner than extrinsically motivated learning (educational psychology).

19

- A healthy, democratic learning community: A prosocial learning community produces tangible educational gains (social psychology).

The multiple psychological disciplines discussed in this chapter provide direct evidence for a resilience education that builds on young people's interests and strengths. To our knowledge, the evidence from these multiple disciplines has not been synthesized into a coherent educational approach. By understanding the principles derived from each discipline and their connections to each other, you will see how resilience education illuminates a clear approach to teaching and learning that promises greater results than individual implementation of any one of its parts.

DECISION-MAKING SKILLS

Nel Noddings (1992) noted that "students may learn better how to learn and may have greater confidence in their capacity to learn if they are encouraged to make well informed decisions about their own education" (p. 286). Noddings's work follows a long educational tradition of the value of autonomy in the educational process promoted by people such as Maria Montessori and John Dewey in the early part of the 20th century.

New and exciting developmental psychology discoveries have shown that these ideas have strong educational merit. It has been found that, when making decisions, adolescents are equal to most adults in assessing life's challenges if they are given proper information (Fischhoff, 1975, 1989; Quandrel, 1990; Quandrel, Fischhoff, & Davis, 1993). By middle school, young people's decision-making skills can incorporate the impact of many influences, such as peers, media, and family (Baumrind & Moselle, 1985; Dryfoos, 1998; Eccles & Midgley, 1989; Eccles, Midgley, & Adler, 1984; Eccles et al., 1993; Jessor, 1976, 1992, 1993; Jessor & Jessor, 1977; Liotts, Jason, & DuPont, 1983). The abilities of young people to make informed decisions are most clearly supported in the landmark Carnegie Report on Adolescent Development, published in 1993, which "challenges longstanding beliefs that adolescents are not competent to make good decisions about a variety of choices facing them" (Takanishi, 1993, p. 86). Takanishi also noted that, when focusing on youth's decision-making capabilities, "the focus is away from the remediation of single problems, such as substance abuse, adolescent pregnancy, and suicide or health compromising behaviors to the promotion of adolescent health or a cluster of health enhancing behaviors" (p. 86).

EMOTION—A LEARNING NECESSITY

If resilience education is to be fully developed, then thinking, feeling, and acting must be explicitly connected in the educational process. Recent brain research tells us that feeling or affect acts as the glue linking thinking and behavior that produces learning (Sylwester, 1995). The psychobiological relationship linking feeling with thinking and learning is promoted in a special issue of the journal *Educational Leadership:* "Thinking and feeling are connected because our patterning is emotional. That means that we need to help learners create a felt meaning, a sense of relationship with a subject, in addition to an intellectual understanding" (Caine, as quoted in D'Arcangelo, 1998). New brain research clearly suggests that for learning to be meaningful, young people must make an emotional connection with their education and their educator.

Before affect was physiologically shown to be a necessary part of meaning making, an educational approach termed *confluent education* promoted the integration of affect with thinking and acting. George Brown (1972/1990, 1975), the founder of this field, described confluent education in this way:

> Confluent education takes into consideration and explicitly uses the emotions, feelings, fantasy, and imagination of the teacher and students in the interaction of teaching and learning to make those activities personally meaningful, thereby expediting and enriching the learning experience. (Brown, 1972/1990, p. 33)

For more than 30 years, confluent educators in fields as far-ranging as religion, business, health, and education have been developing educational processes that integrate emotion, thought, and behavior. The recent linkages between emotion and learning (Goleman, 1996, 1998) have led to a reexamination of confluent education as a promising educational approach (J. H. Brown, 1996; Cline, Necochea, & Brown, 1999). Many of the resilience education strategies in this book draw directly from and build on the theoretical models and research in confluent education.

BUILDING ON INTERESTS AND STRENGTHS

Tapping into the intrinsic motivation of students develops competence and promotes a positive attitude toward learning. Skilled teachers have always used the interests of their students to bring the required curriculum to life. These educators understand that young people are deeply motivated to be "searching for coherence in their environment; that they are constantly striving to make sense of the social and physical world that surrounds them" (Watson, Battistich, & Solomon, 1997, p. 573). Holding this principle as central to the transformative process of teaching and learning requires the educator to carefully engage students' intrinsic motivation for learning. Deci and Ryan (1985) found that those young people who worked to accomplish tasks they themselves had initiated often worked longer and with greater concentration than those who were motivated by external pressures and enticements. Kohn (1996) supported this finding but also found additional and more disturbing effects. Students who originally were motivated to work on their own, when given rewards for their efforts, lost interest in their task when the rewards were withdrawn. This finding suggests that the inherent characteristic of meaning making that all young people are born with can often be undermined, if not wholly obscured, by the sense that personal interest—young people's own internal drive to know and understand—is irrelevant to their learning. Educational psychology research has now clearly established that intrinsic motivation is essential to education. By focusing education away from internal interests, we are undermining young people's natural proclivities toward learning.

Taking a resilience approach often means retrieving this lost sense of personal meaning making and the intrinsic drive to learn. An educator who wants to strengthen a learner's resilience has to understand where the learner is in relation to personal effort and interests. Once an interest in knowing is rekindled, it must then be supported with a purposeful building of strengths and greater internalization of how strengths and interests lead to building a vision of the future.

A HEALTHY LEARNING
COMMUNITY

The previous sections discuss decision making and the connection between emotion and meaning making in the learning process. Educational psychological research connects the intrinsic drive to know and understand with the value of building on interests. All of these principles can best be developed in a healthy, caring learning community. In his book *All Kids Are Our Kids*, Benson (1998) conceives of a healthy community as,

> geographic communities that effectively organize social life to consistently promote developmental assets among young people. . . .
> Healthy communities for children and adolescents are places with a shared commitment to care for young people. They are distinguished as relational and intergenerational places that emphasize support, empowerment, boundaries and opportunities. (p. 21)

It is obvious that having a "healthy community" should help a young person grow up well. Benson (1998) actually showed that the more assets that are available to a young person in a given community, the fewer high-risk behaviors that young person will engage in. In the long term, the individual participating in a healthy community will have more long-lasting and significant long-term relationships in both work and home life.

In the absence of a healthy community, the school becomes the most significant environment where a young person develops. Dryfoos (1994) showed that in many ways the school has become *the* de facto focal point of the community. This is based on the increasing number of people experiencing poverty and family disintegration. Dryfoos also noted that for a community to be healthy there is a need for an "integrated" and "collaborative" educational system. Many social scientists and educational planners have suggested this (Darling-Hammond, 1997; Watson et al., 1997). The interesting implication of Dryfoos's research is that in developing the school as a healthy community, she suggested bringing comprehensive child and family health services into the educational setting. By so doing, she began to translate the concept of a healthy community into schools.

Thayer-Bacon and Bacon (1997) situated the concept of a healthy community in the classroom. In their version of a healthy community, which they called a "democratic community," they also recognized caring as an essential element of a thriving learning community: "When people feel cared for and can make other people feel cared about, then the opportunity for a democratic community is more complete. . . . Caring is a necessary ingredient for any community to be a democratic one" (pp. 31-32). Developing healthy and democratic educational communities has produced resilient behaviors. For example, in the Child Development Project, it was found that development of a school as a healthy and democratic learning community precipitated several positive outcomes. When compared with control groups, young people who participated in the healthy democratic community had a fuller sense of school as community and higher levels of internal locus of control, concern for others, and conflict resolution skills (Watson et al., 1997). Actually participating in a healthy community and developing problem-solving skills through an internal locus of control and conflict resolution indicate an individual's capacity to cope with the complex world. Recent findings from a follow-up study (Watson et al., 1997) of the children in high-implementing schools of the Child Development Project showed that the positive benefits hold over time, even when the students are no longer in schools they perceive as caring communities. Such a finding indicates the power of establishing resilience in young children as one of the most comprehensive proactive strategies for meeting the adverse and fast-changing conditions of life.

Reforming schools into healthy and democratic learning communities produces other benefits. The Coalition for Essential Schools (CES) has shown in some of this nation's most challenging educational environments (i.e., East Harlem) that 75% of young people who experience a learning community that they perceive as caring go on to college. This figure is compared with 62% of young people across this nation's public schools (Coalition for Essential Schools, 1999).

Equally important, though, are the apparent mutual benefits for educators themselves. When educators participate in CES schools, their participation in school governance is nearly double the national average. Brown (1999) noted the importance of a mutual educational experience. Participating in a healthy democratic educational environment that does not hide affect "situates the learner and educator together. It solidifies and sustains learning between people" (p. 174). We characterize this phenomenon as a reciprocal relationship.

As was demonstrated in the Child Development Project and in the Coalition of Essential Schools' research, developing a healthy and democratic educational community enhances both traditional and nontraditional learning. It produces a mutually beneficial learning experience. As George Brown (1972/1990) noted, focusing on the development of these kinds of educational communities

> does not imply ignoring more traditional intellectual goals. What is being called for is not a substitution of therapeutic goals for academic ones, but rather a recognition of the child's needs, so that a classroom atmosphere might be created in which the child is far better able to satisfy his intellectual needs. (p. 373)

Creating a healthy and democratic educational community is essential to resilience education. It forms the very foundation upon which young people and adults facilitate the development of resilience. Within the healthy and democratic educational community, young people develop and learn how to develop caring relationships with adults and other young people. These relationships allow young people to safely experiment with making decisions. In so doing, young people discover their strengths and interests, which can then be supported by the educator. Most important, young people develop a sense of possibility and purpose, and life's development process is sustained because the learning experience is a mutual one. The research is clear that a prosocial learning environment is an essential part of developing resilience.

When we talk about resilience education, we are talking about explicitly utilizing affect to facilitate development of decision-making skills in the context of a healthy, democratic learning community. In the early 1990s, Richardson and Gray initiated a resiliency-fostering curriculum. One of many programs claiming to foster resiliency, it is the closest approach to resilience education that we could find. Finally, One of the only resilience programs in which young people were actually part of the curriculum's development. In their program, the goal is "strengthening protective factors and developing a healthy integration of mind, body, and spirit" (Richardson & Gray, 1999, p. 31). This is to be achieved by helping young people "explore their potentials, create a dream, and learn the skills that will help them live the dream" (p. 32). Their curriculum included several factors:

- Understanding the resiliency process
- Discovering each person's own resilient nature
- Discovering foundations of resilient relationships
- Appreciating "the power of the dream"

- Understanding "the resiliency paradigms"
- Developing "resiliency skills"
- Taking a lifelong resilience-oriented path

These factors have been translated into some early results that are similar to those of the Child Development Project and CES research. Based on early pre- and posttest results, young people participating in their resilience-fostering curriculum show more participation, higher self-efficacy, better decision-making skills, and less involvement with outside negative activities. We look forward to their long-term results.

From their work, it is clear that Richardson and Gray (1999) have a deep appreciation for the importance of fostering a general resilience approach. For them, a key part of working in this modality is the development of a general, healthy, democratic educational community, where resilience is fostered by incorporating affect into the curriculum as a way to enhance decision-making skills. Affect is incorporated through their explicit use of young people's dreams and through the emphasis on finding meaning in their life. Affect is also incorporated by experiential involvement, where young people are encouraged to explore their emotions around the adversities they face in their lives. The incorporation of critical decision-making skills is manifested in the unit on resiliency skills. It is also manifested through the students' own participation in the acquisition, development, and evaluation of the programs. Richardson and Gray's work is noteworthy because it is one of the few programs actually incorporating key evidence to develop a resilience curriculum.

There are several key distinctions between the resilience-developing process Richardson and Gray (1999) have developed and what is proposed in this book. First, resilience education is focused on development in all situations, whereas Richardson and Gray seem to focus on overcoming adversity. This is an important distinction, because educators might continue to assume a deficit view of young people before failure is actually manifested. The positive ways in which Richardson and Gray work with youth somewhat mitigate this. Nevertheless, as is so often the case, the translation from ideal program into practice presents the possibility that adversity and labeling will again distort a resilience "program."

The second distinction we make between resilience education and the Richardson and Gray (1999) program is that here resilience education is directed toward creating classrooms that develop a lifelong process for learning; it is not an add-on curriculum, as Richardson and Gray's program is.

Finally, resilience education as we have conceived of it draws from a 30-year lineage of strength development in education. Before the potential for resilience in education was formally conceived, confluent education was developing the role of affect for learning and decision-making skills, both in the context of a healthy, democratic learning community. This book represents edification and solidification of general resilience principles as they connect with a long-standing educational tradition that operationalizes the values of respect, autonomy, and empowerment of young people in the service of learning and acquisition of a lifelong process for learning.

RESILIENCE EDUCATION, DESCRIBED AND DEFINED

The evidence has come full circle. Not so ironically, caring in the classroom and school community is akin to developing the connectedness discussed at the beginning of this chapter as a key resilience protective factor. Many researchers and practitioners have discussed protective factors in various ways. Programs have been developed in support of them. Yet few researchers or practitioners have made the connections as described in this chapter. We summarize the support for a resilience education model.

Decision-making research supports a cognitive element of an integrated learning process, because its focus is on development of the rational basis for making decisions. By having the responsibility to make decisions, young people internalize the profound sense that they have some measure of personal control in their lives. The "emotion and learning" section supports the idea that emotions are the matrixes through which thinking obtains a felt sense of meaning. Substantial neurobiological research supports the linkage between emotion and learning. When we build upon each person's interests and strengths, we capitalize on his or her intrinsic motivation to learn. From this research, we find that aspects of education too often considered peripheral to teaching and learning or too "touchy-feely" for the comfort of unskilled educators now need to be understood as essential to supporting resilience development. It is in the context of a healthy democratic learning community that young people not only survive but also learn to thrive.

There is ample evidence that each of these individual research areas produces tangible educational benefits. Because it synthesizes what we know about promoting the development of both educators and young people, weaving these knowledge areas into a cohesive resilience educational model holds practical and scientifically sound promise.

In light of the evidence, the goal of resilience education is to develop each person's strengths and interests so that lifelong learning and thriving can occur. This is achieved through developing connectedness in the context of a healthy democratic community. *Resilience education* is defined as the development of decision-making and affective skills within each person and connectedness between people in the context of a healthy democratic learning community. We used the Principles of Resilience Education to develop this method.

Box 3.1 *Principles of Resilience Education*

1. Use strategies that engage students' intrinsic motivations.
2. Allow young people to safely experiment with making decisions.
3. Help create life goals, "a dream" that the learner endorses.
4. Create a "healthy, democratic, educational community."
5. Encourage the exploration of emotions related to the adversity young people face.

II

THE PORT-ABLE APPROACH TO RESILIENCE EDUCATION

IN THIS PART OF THE BOOK, we move from theory into practice. In the five following chapters, the PORT-able approach to resilience education is developed in detail. The first chapter is an overview of the basic principles with some examples. The four subsequent chapters describe each of the model's elements in more detail. As these chapters progress, we hope to get you more involved in resilience education. In Part I of this book, we offered you the choice to skip Part I. In Part II, the choices you will make are within the chapters. Enjoy reading and experiencing them.

4

Educating Through Participation, Observation, Reflection, and Transformation

THE RESEARCH SUPPORT for resilience education, described in Part I, is conclusive. The long-term, convincing, and scientifically sound results converging from diverse yet related lines of research suggest principles that can guide practice. Up to now, the research areas and the guiding principles have not been applied to educational processes. Most remarkable about the convergence of evidence for resilience education is that it gives educators an opportunity, if not the responsibility, to shift how they perceive, act, interact, and react with young people. With resilience education, the emphasis shifts from a focus on adversity to a focus on possibility, or from inabilities to abilities.

In this chapter, we begin with a general overview of the model derived from the principles and assumptions described in the previous chapters. In subsequent chapters, specific strategies and exercises to facilitate resilience in young people are suggested.

RESILIENCE EDUCATION: THE PORT MODEL

How is resilience education brought to life? By using an ongoing, empowering, and participatory process, you—the educator—and the students with

---

Box 4.1 *The PORT-able Model*

> **Participation.** Authentic active engagement with knowledge, content, students, and learning processes that is focused in the present moment.
>
> **Observation.** Noting your experiences. Also known as "note taking."
>
> **Reflection.** Interpreting your experiences. Also known as "note making."
>
> **Transformation.** Awareness of and responsibility for an act, process, or instance of change.

---

whom you work bring the principles of resilience education to life. The word *PORT-able* is used as a descriptive acronym for this dynamic process. We call the process PORT-able because the elements of resilience education can be applied in any learning situation, including schools, classrooms, after-school programs, or neighborhood-based organizations. The PORT-able approach can even be applied to families.

The goal of resilience education is to identify and develop young people's interests and strengths so that lifelong learning and thriving can occur. This goal is expedited by developing the decision-making skills of young people and by employing affect for learning in a healthy, democratic, educational community. Using the PORT-able approach helps you make explicit, develop, and build on your own and your students' interests and strengths. The acronym *PORT* refers to a way of thinking and being with your students that includes four distinct elements: Participation, Observation, Reflection, and Transformation.

PORT is our resilience education acronym because it makes explicit a flexible and empowering educational approach. This approach enhances educators' and students' scopes of vision so that strengths and interests can be identified and developed. It is flexible, because you can do many different interventions as you implement these elements. The interventions that you use depend on your own professional expertise and the choices that you make relative to others and your educational context. As we stated earlier, that may be the classroom, an after-school program, your home, or your neighborhood, depending on your own role in relation to learners. The PORT-able model is empowering in that *you* choose when and how to implement each of these elements. We offer, explain, and provide examples of these elements and how we might implement some of them. You are en-

Figure 4.1. Resilience education: An ongoing process.

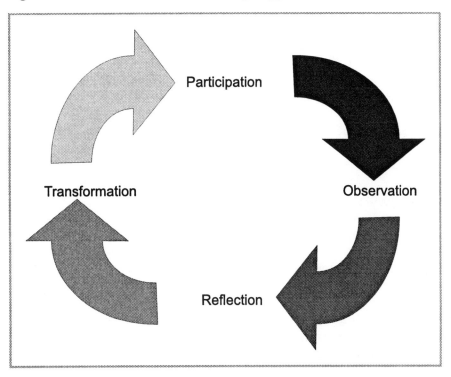

couraged to use your own professional knowledge, your interests, and your strengths to implement the elements of resilience education.

As the elements of the PORT-able approach become integrated into your professional practice, you will be modeling a process for students to develop their own resilience. Box 4.1 summarizes, and Figure 4.1 illustrates, the model. Figure 4.1 describes the PORT-able approach to resilience. The figure reveals that resilience education is not seen as a means to an end. It is an ongoing process, where the means and the ends represent ongoing parts of a cycle of engaged participation. In the following sections, each of these four elements of PORT will be described in more detail.

Participation

Participation, the first element of PORT, involves authentic active engagement with knowledge, content, students, and learning processes that is focused in the present moment. Though you participate in every moment of life to varying degrees, the nature and level of contact you experience with others and the environment vary from moment to moment. The difference between traditional education and resilience education is that you create an opportunity to become more aware of the nature and level of contact at a given moment. You don't go automatically from moment to moment without awareness. Because you learn to experience participation at multiple levels, you are able to make better decisions based on your understanding of your and your students' needs. Participation forms the necessary context for resilience education.

Observation

Observation is the second element of PORT and involves noting your experiences (note taking). Teachers are familiar with observation as a way of assessing students' interactions and work. It is important to broaden and hone these skills. In resilience education, observation is the noting of your experiences without judgment. The key, however, is noting your participation at multiple levels and through the various sensorial modalities. Multiple levels means noting your observations about your personal, internal self, (intrapersonal); what you see happening between people (interpersonal); and what you experience within the context of your environment (systemic). Using multiple sensorial modalities, verbal and nonverbal communication, thinking, feeling, and behavioral information are just some of the modalities of experience that are present at any given moment. Observation is the notation of our experiences at these possible levels and modalities without making immediate judgments.

Reflection

Reflection involves interpreting your experiences (note making). It is critical to separate observation from your judgment about what your observation means, because doing so provides you with moments to distinguish between your perception and your interpretation of your perception. This is where the third element of PORT, reflection, comes into play. Two kinds of reflection can be relevant. One kind is your interpretation of what you are learning about the situation or the content of the learning itself. This is the "what" of experience: what you are learning about how to teach a math problem, or what your students are learning about how to do a math problem. This is the actual level of experience that most people attend to when reflecting. It is termed *content reflection.* In schools, teachers will be familiar with this level of reflection as *assessment.*

The second type of reflection is termed *meta-reflection.* Meta-reflecting on your experience offers an interpretation of an entirely different kind. Meta-reflection is a "step back" interpretation of "how" you experience the "what" or content of the educational situation. The necessary stepping back from the experience while still participating in it allows us to gain insight about the meaning of patterns of behavior and experience. Creating the momentary space between yourself and your experience allows you to make deliberate, conscious choices about how you interpret classroom or familial interactions. Meta-reflection gives insights to patterns of your own interpretations of how students act, interact, or react and, ultimately, insights into how you might intervene. Others refer to this metaprocess as *self-awareness* or *mindfulness* (Goleman, 1996, 1998).

Transformation

Transformation, the final element of the PORT-able model, involves awareness of and responsibility for an act, process, or instance of change. In every moment, there is an opportunity to act, interact, or react. Each of these indicates the transformation of interpreted meaning of an experience into behaviors. In resilience education, *you* create the opportunity to transform participation, observation, and reflection into informed action. When you are participating, observing, and reflecting, because it is along multiple levels and through different sensorial modalities, more alternatives and directions become available. Observation and reflection provide an opportunity to take some time to determine what exists, what experiences mean, and what is important. Thus, in each moment, multiple possibilities for response exist. You can then choose how you want to transform these possibilities into behavior. In transformation, you are aware of your choices in the moment and can take responsibility for the changes you choose.

A brief personal story of transformation might serve as an example. As a child, I (Marianne D'Emidio-Caston) did a lot of climbing. Climbing trees was my favorite, but climbing ladders or jungle gyms attracted me as well. I usually went as high as I could go and then called to anyone within hearing distance, "Look at me! No hands!" I often heard my grandmother say,

"Come down, you'll fall." That was all I needed to hear to motivate an even higher climb. Over time, I internalized an automatic response to anyone's telling me what I couldn't do. My immediate reaction to "you can't" was "Oh, yes I can! Shall I show you?" Once I learned to metaprocess, I recognized how my behavior was controlled just as much by the automatic response to "you can't" as if I had accepted the initial restriction. By taking a moment to reflect, my behavior is no longer an automatic, default challenge of all prohibitions. Between reflection and behavior, there is now a transformation that occurs. It is a conscious, aware evolution in my thinking about the situation at hand. Sometimes my response is the same, to show that something is possible. Other times, my moments of reflection give me the opportunity to say "Not this time." The moment between reflection and action is the moment of transformation that gives me choices I wouldn't otherwise know I had.

The PORT-able model is a dynamic, empowering approach to developing resilience that is applicable to any learning situation. Unlike many static educational approaches, this one is designed to be ever evolving and responsive to what is going on in each moment. With the PORT-able model, you can effectively facilitate resilience education with a group of young people within the often-limited time you are in contact with them. As you use and make explicit your use of the PORT-able model with your students, you will be modeling resilience education for them. As they grow, young people can increasingly use this approach to self-facilitate lifelong resilience. Exercises and interventions that you develop based on the principles and your use of PORT will facilitate your own and young people's resilience.

INITIATING A PORT-able RESILIENCE EDUCATION

The elements of resilience education once considered "peripheral" or "touchy-feely" are now recognized as necessary components of learning, thriving, and developing resilience. George Brown's (1972/1990) acute observation in the context of confluent education should be repeated:

> [It] does not imply ignoring more traditional intellectual goals. What is being called for is not a substitution of therapeutic goals for academic ones, but rather a recognition of the child's needs, so that

a classroom atmosphere might be created in which the child is far better able to satisfy his intellectual needs. (p. 373)

The PORT-able model is directly connected to resilience, confluent education, and related research. The extent of success of resilience education depends on how you develop and integrate the PORT-able elements in your interactions with youth. Developing your skills will contribute to developing resilience in the educational process of your students.

THE TIME FACTOR

It takes time to develop trusting and connected relationships with young people, but time is one of the most elusive of resources in contemporary educational settings. A busy parent struggling to make house payments or a teacher in a high school with 130 students every day continually faces the limitations of time. Acknowledging this is important for two reasons. First, it is the pace of interaction that can often facilitate resilience or undermine its development. Second, recognizing time limitations makes explicit the responsibility of the educator to use time efficiently and effectively. Rapport and connectedness are built when young people have opportunities to voice their perceptions, ideas, and problems with an educator or with peers. To provide such opportunities requires conscious and careful use of the contact time that exists, in some cases moment by moment. One of the most elegant of solutions to this enormous limitation is PORT. We recognize the importance of time and believe that a healthy respect for its value to educators is built into the PORT model. PORT, once learned and practiced, takes seconds to implement. It is dependent on quality of interaction, not necessarily quantity.

ORDER OF ELEMENTS

As you become familiar with the PORT-able elements, the order in which you do them may vary somewhat. Usually, however, transformation into action will follow the preceding elements. At any given moment, the impor-

Figure 4.2. PORT-able theory and practice in resilience education.

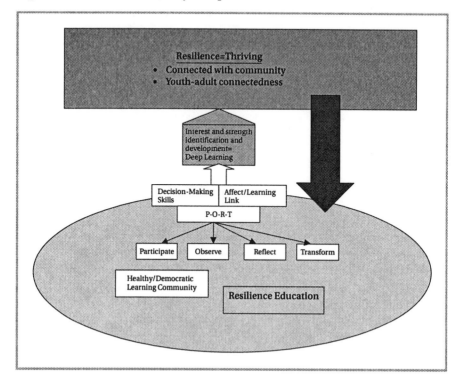

tance of each element may also vary. Based on observation and reflection, your translation into action for each will be different at different times. So, too, will the order and importance of the elements of PORT vary according to your developing capabilities to interpret and develop your own experience and your experience with learners.

Please see Figure 4.2, which provides a visual overview of the PORT-able resilience education approach. We invite you to refer back to this as you read the following four chapters.

If you feel confused at this point, or anxious that you don't easily see the application of these ideas in your work, perhaps stay with the feeling a bit. Practice observation at the intrapersonal level. Attend to where you experience the anxiety or confusion. It is that feeling of uncertainty that often takes place before learning. As Brown (1999) noted,

> Uncertainty plays a key role in learning in both the scientific and therapeutic communities. In the latter many find that affective un-

certainty accompanies the process of purging ourselves of discon-
certing internal information (Brown, 1969; Perls, 1988). Affect paves
the way for new information to emerge and become learned.
(p. 172)

This passage only hints at our mutually developing construction of resilience education. Uncertainty, or anxiety as a felt sense, is precisely what
can begin to connect us, the authors, with you, the readers. The text of this
book is our words, organized to share an important educational approach.
How you may experience, observe, or reflect on what is presented is yours.
You may be interpreting what you are observing about yourself as uncertainty. It may take some anxiety or eagerness to move to a new level of
understanding. Reflect on it a bit. Determine through your own reflective
process what your interpretation of your feelings is NOW. Whatever it is, becoming aware of affect is one skill we would like to utilize to facilitate your
resilience education.

Now that you know what you are feeling in the present moment, perhaps you can transform the feelings from your observation into an action.
Perhaps you are ready to turn the page to see what's next!

5

Participation
Authentic, Active Engagement

Around the country, the classroom is coming back to life. Although many educators are responding to standards-driven, prescribed, and static education, enlightened schools are also meeting "standards," but something is different. In enlightened schools, the classes are smaller, educators are teaching in teams, and kids are learning and developing with the educator and one other. Educators are getting to know young people by working with the same students for several years or for longer blocks of time. It is a dynamic, ever-evolving, and empowering learning situation.

The classroom has a noisy buzz. It is not the buzz of a classroom out of control. Instead, the buzz is one of engaged activity. A balance between the educator and his or her students develops young people's natural proclivities to learn and the learning process itself. When educators facilitate young people's own interests and strengths in learning, students discover and develop their own innate interests and strengths. Educators who are "plugged in" know that a key to resilience education is their own authentic contact and relationship with their students. They also know how to facilitate participation between students. The educator also learns and thrives. This is a healthy, democratic learning community—a sustained cooperative with an ebb and flow of mutually empowering participation between educator and student and between student and student, each engaging with him or herself, one another, and the environment.

Some believe that participation, especially the kind described in resilience education, is made up of building blocks, that each action, interaction, or reaction sets the stage for the next. More realistically, though, life

40

is made up of moments when we are in contact with another, others, or our environment. Sometimes there are many continuous moments of contact, whereas others may be a blink of an eye. Sometimes we may be in the presence of others, but not at all in contact. We are "withdrawn," focused on understanding the meaning of the situation. Different levels and kinds of contact are in each person's consciousness at different times. Participation is a series of moments of contact and withdrawal of varying order, duration, and intensity that creates different levels of meaning.

In the last chapter, *participation* was defined as "authentic, active engagement with knowledge, content, students, and learning processes that is focused in the present moment." At any given moment, there are multiple opportunities and points of contact providing an opportunity for developing your own or facilitating others' resilience. Some, many, or all of these points of contact may be directly related to resilience education. The key to resilience education is to be *aware* of the different aspects of participation, how you are doing it at any given moment, and how it relates back to the big picture of connectedness and the promotion of interests and strengths. It is this mindful way of participating that is the essence of resilience education.

AUTHENTICITY AND NOW

The most important aspect of participation in resilience education is an authentic focus in the present. An authentic present focus allows you to be available to the ongoing and multifaceted ways in which you can develop or facilitate resilience education. Two important definitions are:

- *Authenticity* is being genuine with yourself and with your participation with others in various social contexts.
- *Now* is being focused in the present moment.

Within the opportunities of each moment, there is the possibility for furthering resilience education, yet there is also a paradox. Even though each moment is important, resilience education does not depend on any single moment. It is the accumulation of authentic, present-focused moments shared by individuals in the context of a healthy, democratic learning community that develops resilience. For example, students who stay with the same teacher for more than 1 year have the benefit of "know-ing" the way that teacher works. The teacher has the same benefit, building on the former year for connecting new learning to prior experience. With the opportunity to model learning for the younger students, the older stu-dents gain a sense of competence and often develop a compassionate atti-tude of helping. In my[1] classroom, early in the school year, David, one of the students who was in his second of three years with me, was sitting next to a younger student, Loren, who had just begun in my class. David patiently explained to Loren that he could use the construction paper to make a col-lage. He also showed Loren where to get the sponge to clean up the spilled glue drops on the table and told him to tuck his chair in when he was all fin-ished and ready to move to another area to work. A caring relationship was developed between the two boys in a matter of minutes. David and Loren were friends from then on. We use this story to illustrate the importance of using the general strategy of developing authentic relationships over time. Because David "knew" me and what the expectations were in my class-room, he could help Loren, thus initiating a new and lasting friendship.

We have mentioned the importance of authenticity, a present focus, and its role in resilience education. One additional point is noted. Even if you are temporarily withdrawn from contact with others or the environ-ment, an authentic present focus can still be maintained. You may have ex-perienced such moments many times in your own life. You may be talking to a person who says something to you that takes your mind on its own journey. You are in the presence of the other, but you are withdrawn from contact. Your focus is internal. In that case, an authentic present focus means noting that you are thinking about what is going on inside you. Whether in contact or withdrawing from action, interaction, or reaction, participating with an authentic focus in the present moment is a first step in resilience education.

CONTACT

"Contact," however fleeting or enduring, implies significance. The teacher might participate in a prolonged learning interaction with a student who is curious about the nature of electricity. The parent might share just a mo-mentary glance with the child indicating love, warmth, and their spiritual connection. The child reciprocates with an understanding glance. You may be sitting on a beach cliff experiencing the orange-yellow pastels blending into the blue sky. In each of these experiences, in such moments, we are in contact. Even if it is with inanimate objects, fleeting or durable, contact is the aspect of participation that is the vehicle for developing connectedness in resilience. With contact, people connect.

Contact has within it several aspects that we make explicit. We do this so that we can begin to become aware of the multiple dimensions of experience available to us in resilience education. First, contact is relational. Contact occurs in relationship of one to another or even to inanimate objects. Second, contact may but does not have to include mutuality. After all, you can be in contact with a sunset, but others might be concerned if you were to experience the sun responding to you! Finally, contact occurs in verbal and nonverbal communicative dimensions. When we are participating in resilience education, we talk with one another. We also exchange glances, arm movements, and other kinds of body language that are part of our contact. Relationship, mutuality, and awareness of verbal and nonverbal modalities—each of these is part of making contact in resilience education. For resilience education to be effective, though, sustained contact incorporating these aspects is needed. Sustained contact provides the opportunity for a climate of trust in which connectedness, interests, and strengths can be facilitated and developed.

Contact Is Relational

Judith R. Brown (1996) describes contact as "the meeting of oneself and what is other than oneself—other people and things in the environment" (p. 41). Her description asks us to recognize the multiple routes where contact occurs: between a person and others and between the individual and environment. Contact is relational. In 1996 Barott and Kleiveland noted the relative aspect of participation:

> [T]he organism/environmental field is one unit which is dialectically differentiated. That is, "the environment and the organism stand in a relationship of mutuality to one another" (Perls, 1973, p. 17). This idea was taken from the field theory of Kurt Lewin (1935). (p. 69)

These ideas help build our understanding of the role of contact in resilience education. It is the absolute centrality of self—the relationship of self as the central person around whom contact with the environment or with a single (or multiple) individual(s) occurs—in participation that fosters resilient relationships. When we note the relational aspect of experience, we make visible the multiple routes through which contact and participation can occur.

When we then incorporate these multiple points of contact into our experience, the possibilities for facilitating resilience in the educational process become more obvious than in typical participation. We do not describe how they become most obvious, because developing resilience is a general framework in which the application depends on each moment. How you make contact with others or the environment to act, interact, or react in each moment is also unique. When we are aware of the multiple dimensions of contact, we make available to ourselves many additional routes to enhancing resilience.

Contact Can Be Mutual

If one wants to overcome adversities and identify strengths or interests, that person needs to feel that he or she is not alone. Most people need support to acquire the life skills necessary to overcome adversity and to thrive in their lives. This is as true in education as it is in clinical psychology. Contact is that aspect of participation in which bridges of mutuality are built that foster connectedness and empowerment. In addition to relationship, mutual contact is another vehicle for connectedness.

Mutuality is a deeper aspect of participatory contact than relational contact. In relational contact, there can be an exchange, as with mutuality, but there is a key difference. In relational contact, there is the recognition of one related to another, to others, or to the environment. One might note the relational contact that is established when a white middle-class teacher works in a school in a white middle-class neighborhood. Little things are taken for granted on the part of the teacher and the students who share her social status position. Examples she uses to make her points come from the lives of the children. Contact is made and relationship established. In mutuality, there is that recognition, but a reciprocal, supportive relationship is also established and accepted by the involved parties. We can use a similar example of a white middle-class teacher in a neighborhood that is changing from predominantly white to multi-ethnic. What must the white teacher do to maintain relational contact when she doesn't come from that experience? How can she establish contact with the parents or the children from these different ethnic backgrounds? Knowing her students is crucial.

Knowing their neighborhood and their playgrounds or after-school haunts and knowing their parents' frame of reference for schooling, for the use of time, and for language and interactive patterns are all important to achieve relational contact. In both cases, for mutual contact to occur, the educator needs to go deeper into knowing the children. She needs to watch carefully and listen attentively to them speak with one another. She needs to pay attention to which playmates they choose or which toys they bring to share. She needs to know who, if anyone, is there for them when they go home from school. She needs to use the knowledge of the children to design homework, parent nights, and lessons. She needs to want the children to know her as well. And to do that, she establishes a climate of openness and care in her classroom. The mutual understanding of one another is fostered.

Rebecah, one of my student teachers, taught me about mutual contact while she worked on her M.Ed. As a middle-class white woman, working with first-language Spanish-speaking children, she wrote out several of the different strategies she used to get to know the parents of her students. She did home visits, organized a trip to the local university, helped with food drives, and went to birthday parties. She let herself become immersed in the lives of her students to the point that she identified with them from their perspective. She checked up on why her students didn't complete work, and she talked to the parents about it, even if she had to go personally to speak to them. Rebecah cared. Her students knew she cared, and the benefits of mutual connection were achieved. Her students loved school. They were proud to read and write. They tried to please her, and they knew she would know if they didn't put in their best effort. Rebecah benefited from their growth and development, feeling the great pride and humility of a teacher who knows she makes a difference in the lives of her students.

Aside from merely noting its importance as a nuance of participation, the importance of authentic mutual contact is that the mutuality itself often creates new meaning. Let's take an educator-student relationship as an example. Typically, when the educational pedagogy is a didactic one, the educator provides information to the student, and the student appears to be the primary beneficiary. The information that is disseminated tends to be information that is learned and is quite often of little lasting value. In resilience education, though, participation and contact become part of a mutual learning endeavor. This becomes evident in the following passage, written by the educator Aaron Hillman:

> To my great surprise and delight, I discovered that working with students in this program led to accomplishments of my own—my own life and teaching ability were enhanced by the program. I was

learning right along with the students. I became more aware of my students, my surroundings, and myself. (quoted in Brown, 1972/1990, p. 179)

Hillman sees mutuality as a benefit of authentic contact and participation. When he is situated in authentic contact and participation with his students, he is not just giving to them: They are also giving to him. And out of this emerges a new dynamic in which Hillman himself learns something. Here, we see that mutuality is important because it provides meaning and facilitates empowerment. It provides meaning between people so that relationships can be authentically sustained, continuing the cycle of developing and facilitating resilience education. Empowerment is what allows people to thrive despite adversities. It also allows people to soar beyond expectations.

Each of us experiences and engages in creating experience. Each person's experience evolves as a result of participating with another. Mutuality situates people not just one to another but one with another.

Verbal and Nonverbal Participation

Earlier in the chapter, when discussing contact, we purposely mentioned aspects of participation such as deeply meaningful glances. So often, when people talk about resilience, they discuss facilitating it primarily in the verbal modality—fostering connectedness through action, interaction, or re-action between adult and youth or among young people in the context of a healthy community. Several people have recognized the importance of paying attention to and making contact in the nonverbal modality (O'Connell-Higgins, 1994; Werner & Smith, 1982). Geographic proximity of one to another, smiles, frowns, arm, hand and eye movements, and many other gestures constitute essential nonverbal language for contact in resilience education.

Contact that is authentic, present focused, relational, and mutual clearly also occurs in the nonverbal modality. When we pay attention to myriad nonverbal cues, we make available additional ways to make contact. This is similar to our earlier recognition that it is important to make available the multiple points of contact between people as an interpersonal form of facilitating resilience in education. As the book develops, we will pay more attention to the importance of verbal and nonverbal modalities of contact, such as multiple levels and sensorial modalities.

Young people learn to thrive in different ways. Howard Gardner's theory of multiple intelligences opens us to thinking about at least seven different ways of knowing that are directly related to areas in the brain (Gardner, 1993, 1999). Many educators are already familiar with the ideas and use the different ways of knowing as a guide for developing lessons and learning activities for students. By offering lessons through the multiple intelligences, an educator has the opportunity to observe students and get to know their strengths and preferred styles of learning. To develop each young person's interests and strengths requires authentic and present-focused contact. The contact includes attending to the importance of relationship, mutuality, and verbal and nonverbal cues. The explicit facilitation of multiple ways of connecting with others constitutes the contact that is necessary for resilience education. These aspects of making contact allow us to expand our working vocabularies when we participate in resilience education.

The various ways of making contact while participating stimulates the climate needed for resilience education. First, making contact in multiple ways maximizes your likelihood of respectfully meeting young people where they are. Appreciating another's point of view, especially young people's, is the starting point for making inroads on many levels, developing connectedness, and identifying interests and strengths to build on.

Making contact that is authentic, present focused, relational, and mutual, in both verbal and nonverbal modalities, situates us with one another. This is more than just a nuance of contact and of participation. When we are situated together, mutual meaning can be discovered and relationships can be sustained for the long term, thus sustaining the resilience-building process for the long term. Contact, as we perceive it, is the medium through which connectedness develops and through which interests and strengths can be identified and built upon. It is the vehicle of participation to develop resilience in the educational process.

A Climate of Sustained Contact

The educator makes a joke or spontaneously laughs with students. The students respond in kind, also laughing. For some, the laugh is part of a group consciousness. But make no mistake about it. Many young people's laughs are occurring in the context of increasingly diverse and often disconnected familial environments. In these moments, while they may be laughing, some of these students are thinking some of the following thoughts: "Is this a cool teacher I can actually talk to who might listen? Could this teacher help me figure out what I want to do with my life? Is this a teacher who I can tell what is going on with my family and me, or can get help from and not get in any trouble?" Many times, while students are laughing, they are checking you—the teacher—out to see if this joking event is just a random occurrence or part of a long-term classroom climate where you, as the educator, are approachable. They want to know if you will be there when they need you. Students want to know if you will be the adult friend they need to succeed.

Mentoring studies have shown that it is sustained youth-adult connectedness that facilitates resilience. Recently, Bonnie Benard wrote about Public/Private Venture's national evaluation of the Big Brothers and Big Sisters mentoring programs (Tierney, Baldwin-Grossman, & Resch, 1995). Benard (1999) discussed the characteristics of "effective one to one relationships" (p. 94), which included contact of about 145 hours a year, not including phone conversations. In these sustained relationships, the young person believed the mentor "was there," or what we will call "available," for him or her. Where these kinds of effective relationships occurred, young people stayed in school more, felt more competent about doing their schoolwork, achieved higher grade point averages, and delayed their drug use. Sustained authentic, present-focused contact is intimately connected with developing or facilitating resilience. Benard (1994) made the following observation:

> Sustained relationships were those in which the mentor saw him/herself as a friend, not as a teacher or preacher. These "developmental" relationships were grounded in the mentor's belief that he or she was there to meet the developmental needs of youth. (p. 94)

The educator is not typically seen in the resilience-fostering, mentoring role. The contact that is made between educator and student is sporadic, didactic, and all but formal. Typically, this contact is desirous of only one kind of learning outcome: that the student give the answer expected based on the lesson. In the past, the delineation of an educator's role in these typical ways might have been acceptable. However, these are not the sustained, authentic, present-focused kinds of contact that are necessary for resilience education. Today, sustained contact needs to be part of education, because it is the sustained climate of "real-talk" relationships that we now know facilitates connectedness and the acquisition of information as well as a lifelong learning process. Thayer-Bacon and Bacon (1997) described these authentic, present-focused moments and this climate as one where "real-talk" takes place. We maintain that those sustained moments of real talk, of authentic and present-focused contacts, are essential parts of resilience education. This is what we mean by being an adult friend: making sustained authentic and present-focused contact with the young person. Sustained real-talk relationships help young people acquire the tools necessary to comfortably adjust to the rapidly changing world.

On another day, before or after class your student may approach you with some of the life questions he or she is concerned about. The kinds of questions young people may ask depend on their age and developmental level. Nevertheless, in contrast to the model of the educator responding only as an information giver, the moments when a young person comes to you with "issues" are opportunities when connectedness can be established. Interests and strengths can be facilitated. It is the combination of these moments, as well as the sustained overall climate of support, that can lead to learning.

Sustained contact does not necessarily mean constant contact. Given the amount of time educators actually spend with students each year, it does not even necessarily mean more contact. Rather, in resilience education, sustained contact means a shift in educational process so we make higher-quality contact with young people. The educator is not a therapist, but sustained authentic contact lets students know that the educator is available to them. The connectedness that fills the void between student and teacher allows for learning to take place. As you will see later, even if at first nothing appears to be occurring in the traditional sense of education, the sustained availability of that educator to that student sets up the possibility for learning and the student's acquisition of a lifelong process for learning. It creates the conditions for resilience via deep learning, because through sustained authentic and present-focused contact, more strengths and interests than might normally be revealed to the educator are revealed. Sustained authentic contact provides the educator with more inroads to facilitating competencies.

Authentic sustained contact is more than the action part of being available to students. Authentic sustained contact is not more contact, but a classroom climate of contact that properly acknowledges the value of caring as an explicit part of learning and developing young people's resilience.

WITHDRAWAL

All people need a little bit of time for themselves. In some instances, time for ourselves means being removed from the situation, removed, even if only temporarily, from the challenges and pressures of everyday life. This is the psychological shelter that many of us need from a current situation. Here, withdrawal can be represented on a continuum, with an unhealthy psychological break on one end and on the other end of the continuum a healthier aspect of resilience, coping with adversity by disconnecting from extreme adverse external experiences. Complete withdrawal from a situation may occur at times. It may even be a constructive withdrawal. But because we are disconnected from the situation at hand, complete withdrawal is not part of participation in resilience education.

In other instances, we withdraw to reflect on the current experience. Within these moments when we withdraw to reflect, we may be right in the middle of participating in resilience education: We are still participating. Withdrawn moments of participation in resilience education are ones in which contact with others or with the environment is temporarily broken so that the participant can examine his or her own patterns of thinking and feeling. During a withdrawal phase, we can reflect on several things: What are we observing (observation)? What is the meaning of what we are observing (reflection)? What do we want to do now (transformation into action)? Each of these factors is so important to resilience education that each will be elaborated on and demonstrated in the following chapters.

If contact is the vehicle for connectedness in participation, then withdrawal is its power plant. In other words, contrary to what some might think, withdrawal can be generative. At first, withdrawal is the place within ourselves that gives us perspective, where we can clarify meaning. This in turn assists us in marshaling our emotional and/or physical resources. By this, we mean noting the assets available to us so that we can go forward to make the contact necessary to build resilience in the educational process. Available assets can be within ourselves, such as our own coping skills; assets can be within others, such as identified student interests; or assets can reside within the environment, such as available school resources. Withdrawal offers us a key opportunity to step back, yet, ironically, to generate clarification and the marshaling of available assets.

Withdrawal is also recuperative, in that here, while still participating, even while reflecting, we take time to step out of the immediate experience, giving ourselves a little break from what is happening around us to focus on observation and reflection. This is different from the continuum of complete breaks described earlier in the chapter. Here, the break remains with the purpose of reflecting on how to identify and facilitate our own or others' interests and strengths. As we contemplate, because we are perhaps one level removed from the situation but still participating, we can recuperate.

PARTICIPATION IN RESILIENCE EDUCATION

Participation is the specific aspect of the learning process that allows resilience to be facilitated. It includes phases of both contact and withdrawal. During contact phases, we participate in relationships of one to another, to others, or to the environment. Contact is the vehicle for achieving a feeling of connectedness. We recognize that participatory contact can include mutuality between people, where mutuality is an acknowledged connection between people. Contact can be made in both the verbal and nonverbal modalities. Participation in resilience education is best served when contact is sustained by a supportive climate that includes many moments of contact. As important as sustained contact is, withdrawal is equally important. When we withdraw to look inward, we can clarify meaning and then marshal our emotional or physical resources.

Participating in these ways does not necessarily mean more participation. Most often it means more effective kinds of contact that include an ongoing awareness and explicit utilization of the factors described in this chapter. The sum total of these experiences builds a mutual understanding of interests and strengths and thus connectedness. As part of an ongoing cycle, connectedness becomes simultaneously the stimulant and the vehicle for empowerment, learning, and thriving. Participation is indeed *the* key context of resilience education.

NOTE

1. While "I" may refer to any or all of this book's authors, Marianne D'Emidio-Caston provided the classroom stories illustrated throughout the text.

6

Observation
NOTING YOUR EXPERIENCE

SMALL GROUPS OF STUDENTS clustered together, interacting with each other, problem solving, brainstorming, or discussing an idea the teacher has presented to them is a familiar sight in many of today's classrooms. When we look closely, there is another familiar sight. Three of the four clustered students are eagerly engaged in an interaction, and one of them is sitting back in her chair, arms crossed, rocking back and forth, and then allowing her head to collapse into her arms. Now her head is down on her desk, and the other students apparently take no notice. A teacher, carefully monitoring certain aspects of the situation, observes the group, approaches the table where they are working, and says to the student with her head down on the table, "Why aren't you helping the group solve the problem? You should be helping them!"

In the context of that class, the young people, and that moment, the educator obviously saw fit to do what she did. It seemed an immediate reaction to the situation. It was probably an authentic response to that situation based on the objectives the teacher had for participation in group work. Before making a judgment about what *should* have been done, though, what would happen if we put the car in reverse just a bit and asked: "Is this all that we could have experienced and observed? Were these young people laughing at the nonparticipator? Were their faces turned down? Were they smiling? Do you observe one or more students taunting another one? What were the students' tones of voice? What was the context of the interaction? Did the teacher take into account their personal, social, or emotional histories? What patterns of behavior did the teacher bring to bear on her decision to

52

intervene?" Even though the educator was "carefully monitoring certain aspects of the situation," these are just some of the possible observations the teacher could make to provide more information about that situation. This information could be highly relevant to interpreting the situation before a judgment about what "should" be done is actually rendered. This information may or may not change the educator's next steps. The importance of this educational vignette and the questions we asked after describing it begin to tell us how important observation is for resilience education.

We have so many filters in our everyday lives that we often see life only through one immediately focused lens. That lens is always colored and shaped by our own prior experiences, by our insights and values. Perception itself is so biased that philosophers of many traditions have observed that "we see what we want to see and we hear what we want to hear." In our everyday lives, we see and interpret and then immediately act, interact, or react. But in resilience education, we are attempting to more deeply engage, to become more receptive to ourselves and our students. Although perhaps counterintuitive, the key to effective observation is to remove the automatic perceptions, to understand our own biases, and to open up to the multiple possibilities in each moment. Effective observation amplifies the multiple possibilities of how and where we can look to develop resilience in the educational process. Effective observation gives us multiple insights to developing resilience.

In this chapter we discuss several aspects of observation in resilience education. Rather than doing what we have done to this point in the book, simply talking about elements of resilience education, we will occasionally break from what might be considered the normal flow of the book. In these places, we will attempt to more deeply engage you in observation by developing an exercise. The chapter includes two brief exercises designed to tune you in to how observation in resilience education can mean looking at more than what we are traditionally accustomed to look at. In this chapter, within the limitations of the book format, we begin to model resilience education by doing it. Let's get into the details of observation.

Paradoxically, observation in resilience education is where the educator begins to momentarily "step out" of the educational situation to become more fully informed and engaged in that educational situation. Because most interventions occur within seconds of first notice, what we are talking about here is a skill that you can speed up as you are more and more comfortable with its use. Ultimately, nonjudgmental observation provides time to identify your own or others' assets, interests, strengths, or personal biases.

When observing in resilience education, we take the time to look in places and ways that are uncommon to many who haven't learned and practiced the skill. Observation in resilience education includes three key elements: (a) withholding judgment, (b) observing along multiple levels, and (c) observing along sensorial modalities. In reverse order, let's get right into them.

MULTIPLE SENSORIAL MODALITIES OF OBSERVATION

As humans, we see, hear, smell, taste, touch, and feel. These are the multiple sensorial modalities available to you in your practice. How often do you use more than two senses or look at two perspectives of one situation? Observation of multiple sensorial cues includes verbal and nonverbal cues, as described in the participation chapter and in the vignette at the beginning of the chapter. This means listening not just to what people say but also to how the "what" is being said, paying attention to voice intonation and facial expressions as well. Observation using multiple sensorial modalities includes paying attention to the affective response set up by the situation in yourself as well. You see the interaction, but do you pay attention to how others are positioned relative to you, or to what gestures were used to illustrate a point? Given the social lives of children in a classroom, would you be aware of the student who felt left out or isolated from the others? If they had just come in from recess in a turmoil, you would see and perhaps hear it. But would you pay attention to the sounds or vibrations of a low-pitched hum or the blinking of fluorescent lights, which may distract a student from the work at hand? These are just some possible sensorial modalities that we can experience by observation. In resilience education, we look more and more deeply among these sensorial modalities for opportunities to connect with the experience of the students.

The point of this section is to begin paying attention to these multiple sensorial modalities so that you can begin appreciating the possibilities within yourself and students to locate more ways to develop resilience. The more sensorial modalities and dimensions that you become aware of, the more possibilities you have to identify assets, interests, and strengths. The more you begin to appreciate these possibilities with your students, the more connected you will be with them, and so on and so forth.

A LOW-RISK, LOW-INFERENCE EXERCISE

Now we want to conduct what we call a "low-risk, low-inference exercise." These technical words simply mean that despite the limitations of the book, we want to try to engage you in a nonthreatening (low-risk), and non-judgmental (low-inference) exercise that will begin the process of attuning you more and more deeply to the multiple sensorial modalities. For much of the remainder of the book, we will attempt to periodically and experientially engage you. Because you will have experienced these PORT-able strategies, you can continue using them yourself, applying them in the classroom, and modeling them for your students.

When we begin participating in resilience education, we provide ground rules. Although the research literature uses the term *norm setting*, we prefer the more familiar term *ground rules*. Ground rules include but are not limited to the following:

- Participation is voluntary.

- Each individual speaks for him or herself.

- Any personal disclosures made during participation remain confidential.

Setting such ground rules as these provides important information to young people. They help the educator make explicit that this is a unique learning environment, one that might initially be unfamiliar to students but that will become familiar and almost second nature over time. Ground rules also allow each person to be informed about the nature of participation. They provide clear expectations for students' behavior. In the same vein, ground rules begin to set up a respectful climate with students, because they offer choices for participation.

The exercise is now beginning. If you choose not to participate, then perhaps you want to skip to the beginning of the next section. If you choose to continue participating in this experiential literary technique, then we will begin at a very concrete level of observation. Right now, can you observe what you are experiencing in multiple sensorial modalities? How is your body positioned relative to this book? Are you leaning forward toward the book? Are you leaning away from it? Do you see the words clearly? Are you, right now, touching the book? Are you making sounds as you read? Does the paper have a particular smell? Are you experiencing something entirely different? Do your eyes hurt? Take a moment and observe your experience with this present focus. Rather than focusing only on what comes to you, be more deliberate. Observe and experience in each of these sensorial modalities. Keep the observation at a low-inference, descriptive level. When we actually write our descriptive observations, we refer to this skill as *note taking.*

Here is an experience. Right now I am writing. I feel and hear the tik, tik, tikking of my typing. I am seeing the words move onto the screen as I type. I smell coffee. My feet are resting on the plastic-covered floor. I am now stopping typing and crossing my hands. I put them behind my head and reread what I have typed onto the screen. As I return to typing, I move my body position from leaning back to leaning forward again toward the screen. I smell cold tea that is next to my left wrist. I hear the radio playing. These are my immediate observations in multiple sensorial modalities *now.*

Note that each of my observations is very low inference, because I am simply describing my experience of my observations. I am not saying what should be done next or what might be done next. I am giving myself a moment to observe and experience. Here we are simply opening up to the multiple possibilities of each moment, without yet making a judgment as to what they mean.

Now, as your observations are noted, can you reengage in the traditional flow of this book? You will note that in my descriptive paragraph I observed my experience along multiple sensorial modalities. I noted the tactile experience of my feet, my typing, my various body positions and those of my eyes, the smell of tea, and the auditory experience of the radio. It is likely that not all the possibilities that exist in each moment have been experienced, let alone observed. By observational exercises, though, we are beginning to become more attuned to the multiple possibilities for observation available to us at any given moment.

MULTIPLE LEVELS OF OBSERVATION

In addition to multiple sensorial modalities of observation, there are multiple levels of human participation available for our observation. If the sensorial modalities represent how to observe, the multiple levels represent where we can observe. To this point, we have not yet discussed the multiple levels of observation that we can experience. Three levels cover participation in the human experience: (a) the intrapersonal level, experiences within each individual; (b) the interpersonal level, interaction between individuals; and (c) the social contextual level, the environment outside of individual experience and group interaction (J. H. Brown, 1996). Each of these levels represents a possible aspect of participation that is available for our observation.

A note to avoid confusion. When we are actually *experiencing* in resilience education, we are always doing so on the intrapersonal level. That is, every experience that we observe is *our* experience. Even when we are experiencing observations of various contexts, such as a sunset, or interpersonal interactions, such as the student interactions described in the vignette at the beginning of this chapter, we are doing so on the intrapersonal level. At the same time, though, we are observing on these different levels. So, while we are noting observations through our own experience of them, we can tap into not only our experience of ourselves, but also our experience of others or of various contexts. The importance here is in making explicit that there are multiple levels on which to focus our attention and experience.

For some practice, how about another pause in typical writing and a continuation with our literary technique of attempting to more deeply engage you in observation for resilience education? If you do not want to participate, please continue reading at the section entitled "Nonjudgmental Observation." If you choose to participate, then let yourself observe your experience on multiple levels. What contexts are entering your consciousness? Are you reading in the context of a silent room? Are you in a library with the low-level hum of fluorescent lights? Do you feel the vibration of someone cleaning the floor near you? In essence, observe how your surroundings are affecting you. Please take a moment and observe what contexts are affecting you right now.

On the interpersonal level, are there people around you? Do you hear interaction, or are you part of an interaction? If interaction is occurring, is it verbal? If so, what is the voice intonation? Is the speaking soft or loud? Fast or slow? How are the people who are interacting positioned relative to one another? Are they close together, leaning into one another, or away from one another? Note how you experience interpersonal interaction if it is present.

Finally, check in with yourself. As you did in the last section along multiple sensorial modalities, now note some additional self-observations: How are you positioned? Are you eager to try this in your classroom tomorrow? How does your face feel? Are you warm, cold, or just right? Are you hungry? Are you chewing gum?

Now I share some additional experiences. Right now, on the interpersonal level, there are workers immediately outside my office. I cannot see them, but I can hear them. They are talking to one another at a low voice level. Now, they are doing construction. One is sanding wood. The other is jackhammering cement.

On the contextual level, again the radio is playing loud. The jackhammers are interrupting my thinking process. There is a purple watercolor painting of Billie Holliday on the bookshelves across from where I am sitting.

On the intrapersonal level, I am thinking about what I am writing now and what I am going to write next. My fingers have been resting on the computer keyboard, and now I am writing again. I feel a lump in my throat. I swallow and continue writing. I feel an urge to plead with the jackhammer workmen to stop!

Notice how here, in each description of each dimension, we are sticking as close to a description of our observation as possible. In my descriptions, there is no "this means this, that, or the other thing" or "we should have done this or that or the other thing." The descriptions that you and we noted were very close to the experience, free of an immediate judgment or interpretation of meaning. This is the time when we are simply noting and stating occurrences. We are clarifying what is occurring through observation. We are being descriptive rather than evaluative.

Now, we are concluding these brief observational exercises. At this point, ideally, we are more aware of the various ways in which we can observe. You may want to move this into your everyday life by beginning to observe, note, and describe your everyday experiences.

What we mentioned earlier in the chapter is worth mentioning again: Multilevel and sensorial modality observations are critical to resilience education. Observation can help us open the doors to our perception. It can provide us with self-understanding. Observation also helps us identify and facilitate the development of the interests and strengths of our students.

NONJUDGMENTAL OBSERVATION

When we are observing, the closer we stay to observation without a judgment of meaning (note taking), the closer we are to being able to deliver resilience education. In this section, we want to talk more about the importance to resilience education of distinguishing between observation and judgment.

So often when we talk about our perceptions, we note an observation and then quickly skip to an interpretation of it. The tendency is to immediately and almost imperceptibly slip into what something means or what should be done. "Shoulds" are indications of a judgment and a confusion between observation and interpretation. Either implicitly or explicitly, *should* indicates to ourselves or others that we have formulated an opinion about the meaning of an observation and that the next step should be this, that, or the other thing. As Stewart Smalley, the insightful comedian also known as Al Franken, has noted, "When I do this I am shoulding all over myself."

Even more challenging is when one gives the appearance that there is no judgment by telling another something like "I am not telling you what you should do. . . . It is just that this is what I see and I don't want you to fail at this or that or be miserable doing this or that." Once again, there exists an observation and an implicitly linked judgment. We are not using the word *should*, but there is definitely an implicit message that there is a right way and a wrong way to do this, that, or the other thing and that this person holds the key to the other person's success.

On one hand, observation linked with judgment may immediately clarify meaning on one aspect of the observation. The interpretation etches out our position, where we stand in relation to that particular observation. On the other hand, though, it may close the window on other observations, because a judgment of meaning has been made about the situation. And this may or may not be in sync with the people you are participating with in resilience education. They may or may not feel the same way you do or may or may not be ready to hear what you have to say. Linking observation with judgment may enhance resilience, because you have successfully identified or built on limited aspects of your own or others' interests and strengths. Observation with immediate judgment may clarify and build resilience, but it carries with it a high possibility of being premature.

Why is this issue so very important in resilience education? When judgment and observation are implicitly connected and confused, we often see a disconnect between educator and student—precisely what we are trying to avoid. Here, a disconnect is seen as a temporary or longer break in building or existing emotional connections between participants as a result of offering a premature or unconsciously linked judgment. When people make implicit linkages between observation and judgment, this is often the specific place where attempts at resilience education fall apart.

In distinguishing observation from judgment you will become a source for your own clarification of your experiences, as described earlier in the chapter. You will also become a resource for young people because they will perceive you as being able to clearly separate observation from your opinion and as being receptive to their perceptions. This does not mean that you do not have opinions! Although it is an admirable goal, being completely nonjudgmental is usually not really possible. It simply means that you will be able to clearly indicate and model for young people how to distinguish between observation and judgment, which in the next chapter is termed *reflection* or *note making*.

APPRECIATION OF OTHERS' PERSPECTIVES

"You never know what something feels like until you walk a mile in another person's shoes." How many times have we heard this saying? When observing in resilience education, this call for empathy takes on special meaning. This saying is about appreciation of similarities and differences between ourselves and others.

We have seen that effective observation allows you to widen the range of possible routes to developing your own or facilitating your students' resilience. Doing so without judgment allows you to stay open and be receptive longer. Effective observation provides one critical additional benefit. It allows you to begin to appreciate others' observations. You need this, because each person's perception is relative to another's. By observing and hearing others' perceptions, you understand where you are situated. By *appreciate*, we do not necessarily mean that you agree with the other person's observations. Rather, we mean that you understand what is occurring for that other person or those other people. This provides the possibility of working toward meeting your own and others' needs because you are now beginning to understand what they are. In yourself and your students, you can now begin identifying these observations as potential strengths and interests.

OBSERVATION IN RESILIENCE EDUCATION

Observation in resilience education allows us to widen our scope of vision and to deepen our understanding of a situation by doing several things. First, it allows us to widen our understanding, because we are looking toward multiple sensorial modalities and levels. Second, it gives us time to absorb meaning. Third, observation provides the opportunity to appreciate other people's points of view and how we are situated relative to others. Finally, observation provides us with clues as to how we can work with others in ways that are meaningful to them and us.

The heightened awareness emerging from nonjudgmental observation allows us to make resilience more than an occurrence. When we conduct effective observation in resilience education, we continue the participatory shift from happenstance involvement to deliberate forms of involvement. The first part of this shift is authenticity with a "now" focus. Nonjudgmental observation brings experience into awareness. Awareness of your experience through observation allows you to begin the process of purposely making informed decisions about how you can develop your own or facilitate others' connectedness, interests, and strengths.

7

Reflection

INTERPRETING YOUR EXPERIENCE

TO A GREAT EXTENT, resilience education depends on how we understand the meaning of what we observe. In the last chapter, we discussed the importance of distinguishing between observation and reflection. In this chapter, we discuss how our observations can be organized into patterns that form an interpretive framework. Content reflection and meta-reflection are two distinct ways we find meaningful patterns. Each is briefly defined here. Reflecting on the educational subject itself is *content reflection.* Reflecting about the process of developing or facilitating resilience education relationships is *meta-reflection.* An example will help. Part of the reform efforts in mathematics education has emphasized not only the ability of a student to "get the right answer" but the process used to get the answer. Observing the student's work carefully will reveal both accuracy (content) and methods used by the student to obtain that answer (process). Taking a "meta" perspective allows you to understand patterns in the logic the student used to get the answer. It also lets you differentiate and find meaning in the patterns of your own feelings, thoughts, and behavior and in student interactions or your interaction with them.

In this chapter, we are going to develop and work on experiencing content reflection and meta-reflection. We will also facilitate an exercise designed to help you practice observing and distinguishing between observation and reflection. We will use vignettes and exercises to begin reintegrating the participatory and observation skills into what we call "reflective practices." We include examples of these skills in action through vignettes showing how an educator might engage in content reflection and meta-reflection.

An Interpretive Framework for Observation:
Content Reflection and Meta-Reflection

An educator carefully observes students doing math problems in partner groups. As she scans the room, one pair of students catches her attention. She observes that the two have their heads together and are talking with animation about different ways to do the problems. The teacher reflects: "Are they arguing about who will do what and not getting the work done? Are they so enthusiastic about the work that they both want to do it? Are they contributing various ideas to each other that extend their thinking?" She observes for a bit longer before deciding to intervene. Depending on how she interprets their behavior, her intervention will be different. The students decide to alternate, each doing a problem while the other writes what is done, switching after each is completed. They get to work. At this point, the teacher is satisfied that the students are progressing with the task. She waits a bit longer before she checks in with her class to see if they feel they have had sufficient time to do the math problems. Then she brings the groups back together. She asks, "Who wants to show how they did the math problem?" Many children raise their hands. The teacher smiles and acknowledges that they are eager to participate. The teacher looks around and says, "How about giving a chance to someone who has not yet had one? Johnny, how about you showing us how you and Seth did this problem?" Johnny says, "OK, first we added the five to the nine. When it added to fourteen, we carried one over to the next column then added the two plus the one, plus the one we carried over and that equaled four. So, we got the answer forty-four." The teacher listens attentively and among many observations notes that the student did the common addition algorithm and got the "correct" answer. The teacher notes the obvious, that Johnny seems proficient in addition. Her focus is on assessing the student's acquisition of knowledge. This is content reflection.

Content reflection is considered the more common approach to making meaning out of our observations. One further step can be taken with content reflection. The educator notes that in all cases, Johnny used units to represent 10s when explaining his work. Looking for this pattern in other students' logic may give a direction for future lessons on the base 10 system and place value. This second step is meta-reflection on content. It is finding the patterns in the thinking of the students.

The educator makes another astute assessment of Johnny's skills. She selected Johnny because when she asks for a student response, Johnny is not often one who responds (observed pattern). This time, he did raise his hand, and she chose to encounter him when he volunteered to work in front of the rest of the class. She does a meta-reflection on interpersonal development: What was it about this particular time that made the difference for Johnny? Why did he seem so confident today? Was it Johnny's connection to Seth that made the difference? The teacher is "note making" by asking questions rather than making statements.

The educator's interpretation of Johnny's participation in group interaction represents only one level of the possibilities of reflection, the interpersonal level, which was described in the chapter on observation. An educator can, for example, reflect about how she is interpreting her own professional process, how she is better able to see the logical patterns her students use, or her new attention to the attitudes her students display when they work. She may still want to think about how partner grouping or other strategies in the learning community may be affecting the students' experience of group interaction. She may or may not actually follow up on these musings. What is important here is that, in the educator's perception, Johnny's competence in addition and his confidence to share his answer are strengths that he possesses. These are skill areas of Johnny's that the educator can build on.

Some of the most important meaning making occurs when we reflect not only on the content itself but also on the meaning of the educational relationships we experience. When we are engaged in making interpretations or hypotheses about the relationships in which we are participating, we are practicing meta-reflection.

There is an additional point to be made about this vignette. We discussed only one reflective perspective. This vignette represented the educator's introspective content reflections and meta-reflections. As you will see, reflection involves not just each person's introspection but also mutual participation of each person in contact with others. This is important so that we can compare our interpretations with other people's perspectives and points of view.

The Contributions of Reflection to Resilience Education

Reflection provides us with opportunities to determine if young people's interests and strengths are being served. Practicing both kinds of reflection may also tell us if the emotional connectedness needed for thriving is being developed. Let's get a bit more specific about the contributions to resilience education that content reflection and meta-reflection make. As we deepen our understanding of these two distinct kinds of reflection, we will begin some reflective exercises.

Content Reflection

In content reflection, we make the traditional assessments that most educators make about the extent to which students are learning educational material. These assessments are necessary because they help us to know young people's competencies or strengths in various educational subjects and to "diagnose" errors in logic that will lead to further instruction. Content reflection may be seen as the assessment that often takes place in an educator's mind. What does the educator think the student is learning about the subject being taught? What does the student think he or she is learning about the subject? Questions like these ask participants to reflect on young people's strengths as they directly relate to the educational content.

In content reflection, some of today's professional educators are adding another dimension to their reflections on young people's subject mastery. They are doing more than reflecting on young people's strengths. They are also reflecting on young people's interests. An example of this is an easily adapted learning strategy called "KWL." Here, young people are asked to brainstorm what they *know* about a topic or concept. At this phase of the strategy, young people are identifying their strengths by describing their knowledge and related experiences. The students are also asked to share what they *want* to learn or what interests them about the topic. This stage of KWL can be done individually, in partners, in small groups, or as a whole class. They share with the whole group what they know. They also note what they want to know. This constitutes identification of interests. So in addition to showing their strengths, young people are also asked to identify their interests. Reflecting on young people's interests gives us more information about the possibilities for building competence and mastery. The teacher then designs learning experiences for the students based on what she knows about their prior knowledge and interests. The final part of KWL is the presentation of what the students *learned*. Again, this can take many forms. It provides the opportunity for participation once again, as the students share their knowledge and the educator participates in listening and questioning, being present to the students as they express their learning.

By practicing content reflection, the professional educator can obtain a storehouse of information. Content reflection gives us valuable information about how well young people are learning what they need to know in a given subject area. It also gives us a history of the young person's achievement. In many cases, educators add the dimension of getting feedback from students about their interests. Incorporating strengths and interests into our content reflection gives us some important information about what young people are achieving and what they might want to achieve. In resilience education, the evolving storehouse of reflective information about subject mastery and interests is most useful when it becomes part of our ongoing, moment-to-moment experience with students. This is different from dredging up historical information of the past performance of young people and using it to label them or to characterize them by their deficiencies. Content reflection is an ongoing opportunity for assessing strengths and interests of learners. Making this a part of your practice will increase the potential for resilience in all of your students.

A Content Reflection Exercise

Here is a brief content reflection exercise designed to continue modeling the process of resilience education. We begin to integrate participation and observation with content reflection. First, we will make some low-level, low-inference observations. Then we will follow these with some content reflection work.

Setting of Ground Rules. We invite your participation in this experiential exercise. Your reading of or participation in this exercise is completely voluntary. At any time you may stop. If you do not wish to do the exercise, please go to the next section of this chapter.

Modeling Activity: Note Taking. My first step is to share my observations of the moment with you. This is what we term *note taking.* What am I experiencing now? I am not presently engaged in an interpersonal interaction. I am in my office in my home. I smell the coffee near my desk, and I hear the radio playing. On the intrapersonal level, I am experiencing drinking coffee. It is lukewarm as it slides down my throat. The smell is warm and rich. On the radio, I hear a car commercial during Terri Gross's *Fresh Air.* I think about the context of National Public Radio. My lips are pushed together tightly, and my eyes are now looking at the screen. I am thinking about where this book is going and how my colleagues are interpreting this work. These are some of my observations.

Modeling Activity: Note Making. Now, I reflect on these observations. This process is termed *note making.* I am comfortable in this office. The coffee has warmed me, and I decide the radio is a distraction. My most salient reflections center on what I am learning from writing this book right now. I am learning of the tight connection between participation, observation, and reflection. I am learning that it is a challenge to break these elements apart while explaining them. I am beginning to believe that it can be done through this technique of modeling resilience education with you, the reader. I am working on the language to accurately describe resilience education. I am also learning how to describe these elements while conducting an experiential exercise. I experience a hope that I have identified a strength and interest of mine: communicating resilience education practices in ways that will be usable by professional educators.

Take Your Turn. First observe, then reflect. Please take some time to observe on multiple levels (intrapersonal, interpersonal, and contextual) using different sensorial modalities. Check in with yourself. What are you experiencing? Are you reading aloud or silently? On the interpersonal level, are people around? Are you part of an interaction involving kids or your family? Do you observe that various social contexts are affecting you? Is a television on in the background? In whatever form is most meaningful to you, take a moment to note your observations (note taking).

Now, let's move on from observation to content reflection. Try to make explicit what you are learning about resilience education. When you reflect, are you clearer about the distinction between observation and content reflection? Are you asking: "What is this guy's point? Where is he going with this?" Or is your experience somewhere in between? Do you want to try this same exercise in your classroom tomorrow? Try to avoid moving ahead or behind to what was or should be done. Try to avoid getting into the emotional aspects about how the information is being presented right now or how you might feel about the authors themselves. Take this moment to solidify what you are learning about resilience education itself.

Now that you have begun to do content reflection and experience how it might fit in with participation and observation, we want to transition to another, deeper level of reflection in resilience education—from content reflection to meta-reflection. We will do this by noting some of the limitations inherent in traditional aspects of content reflection.

The Limitations of Content Reflection

Although some educators include young people's interests in their reflections on student work, content reflection is usually confined to assessing students' content mastery. Interest identification is a key part of resilience education. Yet its general absence in educational settings brings up an essential point that merits additional discussion. In several ways, content reflection leaves us far short of our goal to enhance resilience in all young people:

- Assessment of content mastery does not necessarily give the educator information about the interests of his or her students.
- Important patterns of classroom participation are not made explicit, including each student's preferred learning style.
- Insights on how the educator's practice facilitates resilience in each young person are implicit, not explicit.
- The reciprocal nature of resilience education between educator and student is hidden.
- We miss the "what" and "how" of creating a classroom climate for enhancing resilience.
- Incorporating the emotional dimensions of learning is left to those who are confident in dealing with "charged" human interaction.

The limitations, noted above, of a sole focus on content reflection require more discussion. You will see why it is necessary for a deeper kind of reflection. We have already discussed the first bulleted item. Now we will briefly discuss the remainder of them.

Important patterns of classroom participation are not made explicit, including each student's preferred learning style. We want to know about the student's acquisition of content knowledge, but we also want to reflect on other strengths. What learning modalities does the student use most often? In what contexts? Does the student rely on visual or oral information? Does the student have musical or kinesthetic intelligence? Strengths like being a group leader, accepting feedback, and following directions are just some of the necessary skills needed to acquire a lifelong process for obtaining knowledge. Explicitly reflecting on these kinds of strengths in each young person means reflecting on the patterns of participation that the educator and young people are engaging in during each moment of classroom time. Reflecting on students' participation strengths may be most directly connected with longer-term thriving, because these strengths indicate that the young person knows how to fulfill his or her needs. Explicit reflection by both students and educator on the existence of these skills might reveal strengths that fall outside the bounds of content reflection.

Insights on how the educator's practice facilitates resilience in each young person are implicit, not explicit. If educators identify only student mastery in a subject, how do we know which part of the lesson facilitated that mastery? If we ask students, "What helped you learn this material?" or "What made it more difficult?" the students can give feedback to the educator, which can be built into later lessons and learning activities. Without such a feedback loop, how would we know what in our educational process could be done to further develop the students' growth? Content reflection leaves us wanting more information about what specifically in the educator-student or the student-student relationship facilitates knowledge acquisition, strengths, interests, and connectedness.

The reciprocal nature of resilience education between educator and student is hidden. The traditional goal in much of education is student mastery of learning subjects. Content reflection usually says little or nothing about the reciprocal aspect of the educator-student relationship. We want to know more about (a) what the educator is learning about his or her own practice, and (b) what the educator is learning about creating a general climate of resilience in the classroom. Gaining the insight that comes from reflection on these issues helps us immensely in resilience education. It keeps educators from burning out because they make explicit a lifelong commitment to professional development for their own and their students' benefit. Educators come to understand how they are growing.

We miss the "what" and "how" of creating a classroom climate for enhancing resilience. Explicitly reflecting with students also allows the educator to share the responsibility of learning with students. To the most reasonable extent possible, students are situated with the educator. Situating the educator with the student contributes to a mutual and positive learning climate in which connectedness can be developed. In traditional education, content reflection does not often recognize the importance of the reciprocal relationship between teacher and student.

Incorporating the emotional dimensions of learning is left to those who are confident in dealing with "charged" human interaction. A final issue we face in practicing only content reflection may be the most important one. In traditional content reflection, the focus is clearly on "the facts": Can the young person complete the math problem? Can students decode and comprehend written text? These "facts" are critical for the professional educator, particularly in this time of high-stakes testing. To varying degrees, though, emotion is always present in the classroom. The question is how can we utilize it to the mutual benefit of educators and young people? Developing resilience in the educational process requires paying attention to the emotional issues and patterns of interaction that create classroom climate. Students who have conflicts with friends or family, who feel shy about speaking in English but know the answer, or who believe that being smart will alienate them from their friends are not using their best potential. They are not focused on the present, learning with all of their available strengths. Without attention to the feeling component of learning, these children miss out. In resilience education, attention to emotions is tightly linked to the connectedness needed for thriving.

Even with these limitations, we recognize that content reflection is useful in and of itself. It allows us an opportunity to reflect on the developing strengths and sometimes interests of young people. Knowing its shortcomings mobilizes our energy to do deeper reflection on how we know the young people in our care. Deeper reflection helps us figure out how we can facilitate each individual student's strengths and interests within the context of required lessons, develop a resilient classroom climate, and discover how our own resilience-building capacities are an important part in young people's development. Each of these possibilities leads us to the kinds of reflection found in meta-reflection.

Meta-Reflection

A Meta-Reflective Exercise

Instead of doing more explanation, we want to start this section with an experiential meta-reflection exercise. As always, we invite your participation. Your reading of or participation in this exercise is completely voluntary. If you do not wish to participate, please go to the next section of this chapter. Discussion of meta-reflection follows this reflective exercise.

If you choose to participate, check in with yourself. What are you experiencing at this moment? Now, instead of our offering a number of questions intended to prompt you about the areas in which observation can occur, look along the multiple levels and sensorial modalities and note your most salient observations about what is going on right now. When you feel ready, move on to the next paragraph.

Now, note your content reflections. What are you learning from what we will call the "task" at hand, reading this book? What do you think you are learning about resilience education? Can you share this learning with yourself or a friend? If you share with a friend, try to pay attention to how you solidify your learning. Is it on paper? Do you take notes on what you are reading and show the friend? Do you tell the friend about it? Or do you try to have friends read what is intriguing to you? Take this moment to make notes regarding the task of reading this book right at this moment.

Staying in the moment, can you now begin to let go of what you are learning about the subject of this book? Check in with yourself again, noting your observations of this moment. Instead of what you are thinking about what you are learning, see if you can reflect on how you are feeling about the ways in which you are learning. What is your judgment about the presentation of this book? Do you feel comfortable with it? Do you feel that this book is more deeply connecting you with us? Or does the writing of this book cause you to experience something else? Are you feeling clear or confused, connected or disconnected? Take a moment and "process" your feelings about how the book is being presented to you.

We are limited by the traditions of book writing. If we were together and conducting a workshop on developing our resilience education skills, we might offer some of our own observations and reflections. One of us might say "I see that when I write about issues in meta-reflection on the chalkboard you shift your position in the chair [observation]. I interpret this as you being excited about these issues [meta-reflection]." I could also note how various social contexts are affecting me, or how I feel when you react this or that way to me. You could react by acknowledging my impressions and by then noting your new impressions. This is meta-reflection while making contact or participating. Meta-reflection could also take place in private, while one is introspecting or withdrawn. One could make journal notes, or use the previously mentioned note-making process. If we frame it in terms of participation, meta-reflection has introspective and participatory dimensions. The key is to use these introspective and participatory modes to develop a "gestalt" meaning of participation based on observations.

By employing observation in conjunction with reflection, we are beginning to reintegrate them. They are each distinct, but they can be integrated. We are also beginning to do meta-reflection. When you feel ready to return to the traditional writing of this book, you can see us continue to ruminate a bit about the nature of meta-reflection in resilience education.

A Description of Meta-Reflection

You have already experienced meta-reflection. Because it gets to the heart, if you will, of the emotional issues involved in the educational process, we think meta-reflection is one of the most meaningful and important aspects of resilience education. Therefore, some further description is in order. This will give you more depth on its meaning and importance and also more time to reflect on both. We first offer a general description of the concept of *meta-reflection* and then embellish it with a description more germane to resilience education. The first description comes from the work of Gareth Morgan, an organizational researcher. He developed his example of meta-reflection from the thinking about "cybernetic systems":

> Simple cybernetic systems, like house thermostats are able to learn in the sense of being able to detect and correct deviations from predetermined norms. But they are unable to question the appropriateness of what they are doing . . . More complex cybernetic systems such as the human brain or advanced computers have this capacity. . . . It is this kind of self-questioning ability that underpins the activities of systems that are able to learn to learn and self-organize. . . . Double loop-learning depends on being able to take a "double look" at the situation by questioning the relevance of operating norms. (Morgan, 1986, pp. 87-88)

Whereas we call the process "meta-reflection," Morgan calls it "double-loop learning." You can see that, writing in the mid-1980s, Morgan made a breakthrough with his concept of effective organizations. Morgan saw that a kind of "self-questioning ability" that allows us to "learn to learn and self-organize" is fundamental to successful organizational development. If content reflection represents a single loop of learning, then meta-reflection represents double-loop learning or "questioning the relevance of operating norms."

Judith R. Brown (1996) further specified this concept by generally describing how, in qualitative research, we conduct meta-reflection:

> [I]t is the level where the participants' experiences, their relation-
> ship, and the rules and patterns of the relationship are the matters
> of interest. Paradoxically, to do this one must—momentarily—step
> out of the relationship to bring about a fresh perspective on the
> interaction or relationship. (p. 70)

Implicit in what Morgan (1986) and J. R. Brown (1996) are saying is that a
critical kind of learning takes place in meta-reflection. It is learning how we
learn and learning how to learn. When we conduct meta-reflection, we recognize that changing conditions are ever present. When we challenge our
basic operating assumptions by making ourselves aware of them, there is
an opportunity to adapt to those changing conditions. By doing meta-
reflection, we can evolve with what is actually happening rather than
remaining static regardless of other information.

A description of the way in which evolution of understanding actually
occurs in meta-reflection was initiated earlier. It is worth picking up again.
Our understanding of this process has to do with the participatory phases
involved in meta-reflection, contact, or withdrawal. In her quotation
above, Judith R. Brown (1996) makes the process of meta-reflection visible.
We translate the process from her interest in qualitative research to our interest in resilience education. To do meta-reflection, we must temporarily
withdraw and make contact: "[O]ne must—momentarily—step out of the
relationship to bring about a fresh perspective on the interaction or the relationship" (J. R. Brown, 1996, p. 70). The skill of meta-reflection, which you
will learn by practice, is the shuttling between introspection (withdrawal)
and contact. Contact is reengaging with participants to share a reflection.
An example is sharing your perceptions of how you feel about how your students participate with you (contact) and then listening to students share
their own perceptions about how they feel about their participation with
you. From making your reflections visible and hearing your students' reflections, in the next moment a new understanding based on further observation emerges. Now, through the meta-reflection, a fresh perspective on
the class process is developed. This is the gestalt, the holistic understanding of what is occurring.

Why Meta-Reflection Is Critical to Resilience Education

In science and throughout literature, questioning basic assumptions
and other people's interpretations has been fraught with emotion. So,
you might say then, this is not the stuff of learning with students. Those

interested in adhering to standards might argue that doing meta-reflection and thus incorporating emotion has nothing to do with reading, writing, and arithmetic. We disagree. From a resilience education perspective, nothing may be more important than observing and reflecting on operating assumptions. Nothing could be more important than incorporating those emotions to hear others' observations and interpretations of the educational process. By regularly "processing" or observing and reflecting at the metalevel, we are now serving several important interests of resilience education. We are

- Explicitly creating feedback opportunities so that we can test our assertions about what is or is not working in the resilience education process

- Explicitly recognizing the importance of young people's interests as well as achievement of content learning

- Acknowledging the very real emotions of young people

- Utilizing emotions to create a direct peg for learning and thriving

- Creating opportunities to enhance the educational process in real time

- Providing the structure within which connectedness can develop

- Modeling a process that young people can use to acquire a lifelong learning process

- Testing our own assertions about our own professional growth, which can also be enhanced in real time

In short, if only because meta-reflection builds in a process for making explicit the kinds of learning that are necessary to adjust to changing conditions—similar to the often-changing conditions of a global economy—it is a most important contribution to enhancing the educational process.

Through engaging in the process of meta-reflection itself, we are doing so much more. By participating in real-talk moments such as those that occur during meta-reflection, we are deepening our relationships with students. We are building trust and identifying their and our own strengths and interests. This is being achieved by becoming aware of and taking responsibility for developing our own interests and strengths and appreciating the same from others. As educators, we are freed to act creatively and responsibly by clearly defining the boundaries between our own interests and strengths and those of our students. We are taking care of ourselves and fulfilling our educational responsibilities. By making these kinds of clarifications through meta-reflection, we are contributing to mutual thriving.

Let's summarize where we are right now. In resilience education, reflecting means interpreting the observations we make on multiple levels and sensorial modalities. These interpretations can occur in the form of content reflection or meta-reflection. Whether in a contact or withdrawal participatory phase, each kind of reflection can be used to contribute to resilience education. As with observation, the point worth taking away here is that the possibilities for resilience development, as an ongoing developmental work in progress, become available when we explicitly work with content reflection and meta-reflection. Now, we are nearing the end of this chapter. We have built toward this chapter's final experiential exercise. It will flex our participation, observation, and reflection muscles. It is called the "see, imagine, feel" exercise.

See, Imagine, Feel

In resilience education, we must deepen our connectedness with young people if we are to become aware of and take responsibility for our own observations and reflections. The "see, imagine, feel" exercise is intended to help individuals become aware of their own thoughts, feelings, values, and behaviors; to appreciate other people's thoughts, feelings, values, and behaviors; and to appreciate the way people communicate those characteristics to others. This exercise has several purposes:

- Participating with an authentic present focus
- Becoming aware of your own observations and reflections
- Making clear distinctions between observation and reflection
- Verbalizing without reasons or explanations
- Becoming clear about what is your perception of yourself versus your perception of others

This exercise requires pairs of people or dyads. So if you are sharing the reading of this book with another person, grab that person and do this exercise. If you have a trusted friend or colleague with whom you would like to do this but who may not be familiar with the book, use this as an exercise to begin learning how to facilitate participation in resilience education. In either case, share the purpose (noted previously) and share the ground rules:

- Participation is voluntary.
- Each individual speaks for oneself.
- Any personal disclosures made during participation remain confidential.

As always, we invite your participation in the experiential exercise that is being created. Your reading of or participation in this exercise is completely voluntary. At any time you may stop. If you do not wish to participate, please go to the summary of this chapter. We will now provide enough information to begin the exercise. We will also give an example of distinguishing between seeing (observation of other), imagining (interpretating and projecting possible meaning), and feeling (making explicit emotional aspects of reflection).

John and Mary sit facing one another. Each person takes a turn sharing three sentences. One person begins with the sentence "I see . . ." This person follows with "I imagine . . ." and concludes his or her turn with "I feel . . ." in that order. Mary may begin. She sees John biting his nails or bouncing his leg. Mary says, "I see that you are very nervous right now." But Mary is mistaken: She is not noting her observation; instead, she is imagining that John is nervous. A more accurate descriptive statement that separates factors might be: "I see that you are biting your nails. I imagine that you are nervous. I feel concerned about you." By doing this exercise, each individual becomes aware and takes responsibility for his or her own constructed understanding of the issue at hand. We become aware of the difference between what is actually occurring, what is being imagined, and what is being felt. Try to make sure that your feeling statement is your own feeling in yourself, not your feeling about the other person. Then it is John's turn, and he notes his observations and reflections regarding Mary. Set a time limit to go back and forth a few times. Usually it is about 5 minutes. Wrap up this part of the exercise.

Now on top of the see, imagine, feel exercise, how about if we do some processing in the forms of content reflection and meta-reflection? First, take some time to note your observations about what happened. Now, begin to make some interpretations about what you learned from the exercise. Did you learn the difference between seeing, imagining, and feeling? Did you perhaps become more aware of what is your perception and experience versus what is another's? Each of you take a moment to solidify your learning from the exercise. Perhaps you are ready to share your learning with your exercise partner. If you are, go ahead and clarify and solidify your learning with your partner. Listen to what your partner has to say. This is content reflection.

OK, let's take this to the metalevel of reflection. Make some observations about the present moment. How are you feeling about participating in the exercise? Does its structure make you feel comfortable or otherwise? How did the context in which the exercise was written affect you? Were you focused on the rules of it? Or did you do some improvisation? How would you change this exercise? How are you feeling about the partner you are working with right now? Are you feeling closer to this person? Are you feeling more distant? Check in with yourself and then perhaps share your observations and reflections about this exercise with your partner. Can you hear and acknowledge that you hear the partners' perceptions? What is your reaction to your partner's perceptions? Of these perceptions, what comes into your mind as being most salient? Reflect on the meta-reflective gestalt of the moment. What is the new meaning of the PORT-able resilience process that is emerging for each of you? Now, you are doing meta-reflection.

As we have made clear, the tendency is to briefly observe and reflect and then immediately act. To this point, we have worked with participation, observation, and reflection. The action part of the PORT-able model of resilience education, transformation, will be taken up in the next chapter. For now, we would like to conclude this chapter by clarifying and solidifying some of our own content reflections and meta-reflections.

OUR REFLECTION ON THE CONTENT OF THIS CHAPTER

In this chapter we are developing several aspects of our reflective practices. Reflection is one of the most important strategies of resilience education. In content reflection, we can solidify our observations and reflections about the learning of the subject itself. This identifies our own and our students' strengths. In addition to identifying individual strengths, in some cases, professional educators practice content reflection that involves observing and reflecting on their students' interests. We are learning that content reflection is traditional and essential. The ways in which it is achieved in traditional education may differ from how we do it here. Nevertheless, content reflection provides a storehouse of information that educators need to identify student strengths.

Content reflection leaves us wanting more reflective information to develop or facilitate resilience education. Many of these desires can be achieved by using meta-reflection. In meta-reflection the focus is on learning about how we learn. *We* means not just students but also ourselves. In meta-reflection we reflect on the current educational process by observing and voluntarily sharing our perceptions about how we experienced the learning experience. Meta-reflection serves several purposes in resilience education, which we noted earlier. Meta-reflection

- Purposefully creates feedback opportunities so that we can test our assertions about what is or is not working in the education process

- Explicitly recognizes the importance of young people's interests as well as strengths

- Acknowledges the very real emotions of young people

- Utilizes emotions to create a peg for learning and thriving

- Creates opportunities to enhance the resilience education process in real time

- Provides the structure within which connectedness can develop

- Models a process through which young people can acquire a lifelong learning process

- Tests our own assertions about our professional growth, which can also be enhanced in real time

We have learned that both content reflection and meta-reflection are necessary parts of resilience education. It is the place where our students' and our own interests and strengths can be identified. The process of reflection itself contributes to the development of a positive classroom climate. In working with specific students and with the whole class, the process of reflection can help facilitate the connectedness needed for resilience.

Because it develops each of the above dimensions, we like to make a meta-reflective exercise part of every class day, usually at the end. We will conclude this chapter by offering our own meta-reflections.

We conclude this chapter by offering our own meta-reflections.

META-REFLECTION ON THIS CHAPTER

These are some of our meta-reflections. Right now, we are presenting the PORT-able approach to resilience education. We realize that we have been thinking about how to present this model for months. Let's take this chapter for example. We feel this is a long chapter. Its writing has exhausted our thinking. Should it have been broken up into multiple chapters? We wish we could get some feedback from you, our audience, to see how you are experiencing it. Without your feedback, we tentatively resolve that this is one of the most important chapters in the book. It is a place where several aspects of the PORT-able resilience model naturally intersect. We cannot ignore the overall impression or gestalt that participation, observation, and reflection came together here and now.

Not only are we questioning the layout of the chapters, we are also questioning the experiential literary technique that we have developed and used, particularly in this chapter. We are feeling challenged by shuttling between this experiential technique, vignettes, and descriptions of reflection. At the same time, we are feeling positive. Offering vignettes is good. Offering exercises is better. We conclude that offering possibilities for experience is the best teacher.

We share an emotional desire. We are hopeful that you are learning enough about developing resilience in your educational process that you will continue your own professional development. The actual experience of practicing participation with an authentic focus in the present, observation on multiple levels through various sensory modalities, and reflection on content and meta-reflection will continue to clarify how you can use them in your everyday practice. Practicing these elements will lead to clarity and to the development of resilience within yourself and your students.

From experiencing our feelings on reflection, a gestalt is emerging. In this chapter, we have made significant movement. We are "going from thinking to feeling and from feeling to thinking again, no longer thinking "about" something, but rather a kind of reflection within a field of experience" (Von Schlippe, 1993, p. 210). We feel ready to move into transforming participation, observation, and reflection into action.

Transformation

Being Aware of and Responsible for Change

A Parable

Opportunity is knocking. We ask, "Who is it?" We look through the looking glass door and see that it is our cluster of PORT-able resilience education friends. We open the door and decide to listen to what they have to say.

Participation, the elder sage, is dressed in a buttoned-down collared shirt. He says: "Listen. I can't tell you what to do. I can only share with you what happened with us when we ran our school many years ago. What I learned then is what I know to be even more true today. I am talking *with* you, not *at* you. When we want to reach kids we have to get *real*. To be real with kids we've got to talk with them, not at them, like I'm doing now with you. We've got to talk real. To talk real, you have to be here now. With ourselves and our kids, now is what matters most. To be real, we have got to be here for ourselves and for our kids. Participation is real, participation is here, participation is now. If you want to connect with kids, you've got to get it, you've got to live it."

Observation, the Zen Buddhist in our group, steps forward. He is dressed much like the Dalai Lama. Bald and wearing a golden wrap, he puts his hands together and calmly says in a low, soothing tone: "What we see is filtered through so many doors in our own perceptions. Observation of self is balanced with observation of other. We balance observation of ourselves

80

[intrapersonal] with observation of interaction between us [interpersonal] and various social contexts [social contextual]. We often look with our eyes. We often listen with our ears. We must also balance these senses by hearing with our hearts. We also taste or smell. When we observe we do so with eyes of the child, naive and curious about each new moment, where every moment is one worth observing. By observing ourselves observing, we come to know the patterns of our thinking and how our values influence our thinking." The Zen Buddhist closes with his own clarity: "Observation without judgment gives us a window into ourselves. True observation is with balance of heart and mind and without judgment."

Rabbi Reflection, as he is affectionately known to his resilience congregation, says, "Oh yes, observation is important, but what does observation mean?" He stops for a moment, strokes his long gray beard, and reflects on his original question: "If you are looking for me to tell you what your observation means, how should I know that answer? The only thing I know is that you are both right! Decide for yourself what your experience means. Reflect on what it means. On the one hand, maybe what something means depends on what we find out about the subject. So, the one who takes this point of view is right. Maybe our observation is telling us something about what we are learning about fixing the immediate problem [content reflection]." Ever the wise rabbi, he continues: "On the other hand, maybe there is something deeper in our lives. Maybe our observation is telling us something about our relations or relationships inside ourselves and between ourselves and others, learning about how we work alone and together to fix problems [meta-reflection]. The one who has this point of view is right too! What something means," he says, "is not only up to me. That is why each person is right! It's up to each of us together and alone to make meaning." With his brow furrowed, he concludes: "Reflection on our experience is a process. The answer is not only in 'the answer' itself. Maybe the answers are also in the asking of the questions."

When you invite "The Opportunities"—Sage Participation, Zen Buddhist Observation, and Rabbi Reflection—into your classrooms, you extend your understanding of what we mean when we say that opportunity is knocking.

As individuals and as a group, these three characters give you an image and a chance to conjure up your own character in this parable, transformation in your self, students, classroom, or school. The possibilities for you to characterize transformation are here because of the opportunities: participation, observation, and reflection. The options for transforming possibilities into resilience-oriented actions are now becoming clearer. That is what this chapter is about: two kinds of changes you can make that build resilience and all its benefits in the classroom. The transformation we are talking about is making available the opportunities for change.

TRANSFORMATION THROUGH
TWO KINDS OF CHANGE

So here we are. We are participating, observing, and reflecting in order to develop resilience education. Now different kinds of possibilities for acting, interacting, or reacting are emerging. We can choose to continue teaching exactly as we have been doing. Or we can make two very different kinds of change, which are described by Wátzlawick, Weakland, and Fisch (1974), some early change theorists: "There are two types of change, one that occurs within a given system which itself remains unchanged, and one whose occurrence changes the system itself" (p. 10).

In the first kind of change, we can make some minor adjustments in what we are doing. The fundamental resilience education assumptions and practices that we are using do not change. A resilience education example of this at school might be agreeing with our students' feedback that we need to have more time for physical education during the day; at home, an example might be agreeing that they will brush their teeth before the nighttime story, not afterward. Minor changes in practice that do not affect the system itself are termed *first-order changes.*

In addition to making minor changes, we can make change that involves a fundamental shift in the assumptions and operating processes of our work with youth. This is *second-order change.* An example of second-order change might be implementing a developmental discipline model that regards the misbehavior of young people as an opportunity for learning and building caring relationships. Classrooms that have class meetings built into the structure of every day or at least every week, so that students can talk to each other about teasing, exclusion, or competition, have created one strategy for second-order change.

A quick story demonstrating each kind of change comes from George Brown (1972/1990), who retells the story of "The Princess and the Frog." The frog wants to be more appealing to the princess, so he wears a gilded suit of clothes. This is first-order change. In this scenario, the frog is still a frog. The princess, when she sees this beautiful new suit of clothes on the frog, kisses the frog, and he becomes a prince. Becoming the prince is second-order change!

WHY IT IS IMPORTANT TO LEAVE THE CHANGES UP TO YOU AND YOUR STUDENTS

Telling you what specific changes should be made would be contrary to the goals of this book and ultimately harmful to you and your students. Throughout this book, we have developed a resilience education orientation that can be applied dynamically to any educational situation. Offering specific changes rather than a framework for thinking about specific actions to be taken would send us backward to a static model in which the educator and the learners are not seen as individuals with unique qualities, strengths, and interests. In short, telling you what specific teaching changes *should* be made detracts from what we believe it means to be an educational professional. Instead, through the development of participation, observation, and reflection skills, we encourage you to independently and creatively transform your knowledge of each of the young persons in your care into action.

Offering specific changes that should be made in your classroom would not only be a static professional model but would also be impractical. In any given educational situation, there are so many possibilities for change that we could never cover them in one book.

Finally, telling you how to change would take away from the development of shared responsibility. We discussed the importance of mutuality for facilitating resilience among educational participants. Telling you a specific set of actions to take reduces the potential for connectedness that develops when students and educators determine and engage in the process of making change together.

A LEARNING VIGNETTE

Here is a vignette demonstrating the differences between first- and second-order change.

The children in one classroom I observed were bitterly competitive with each other. Rarely did the teacher acknowledge their abilities, spending much of her time criticizing their behavior with each other and angrily chastising them. As a coach, my job was to help this teacher change the dynamic that was taking so much time and energy from the actual learning that could have been going on but wasn't. When we first met, I asked the teacher to tell me how she felt about her classroom, starting with whatever came to her mind. Her statements were deeply critical of herself: "I have no energy for the children this year. I don't know what to do with them. I try to invent interesting lessons for them, but we can't ever get to them because I can't get them to stop talking and fighting with each other. I leave school every day so tired. I never have time to work on my room either. It is getting piled so high with their work that I haven't had time to correct, and the mess just keeps getting worse. I'm sure the environment is contributing to how the students feel in my room."

First-Order Change

We brainstormed possibilities for action that the teacher could take that would help her and her students feel more comfortable in the classroom space. Perhaps creating some order in the environment would be a starting place. The teacher agreed to spend one or two afternoons during the next week staying at school 1 hr later to work on her room. During that time she tidied up the piles. She threw out some of the old projects that had long since lost the students' interest and rearranged the tables and shelves so the students could walk around each others' desks without knocking into them and therefore could find the supplies that they needed. When the students came to school after each of the afternoon clean-up sessions, they brightened up as they entered the class and made comments such as, "Look how neat it is. And we can find stuff!" Hearing the compliments, the teacher also brightened. It was worth the time she had taken. It felt better to be in the room with them.

The educator's taking the step to clean the room was a first-order change. She made changes that were important but that were not fundamental changes in how they worked together. It produced the positive result of the educator's and the young people's feeling better about their class. This first-order change may also trigger second-order change in the classroom. Let's continue the vignette.

Second-Order Change

The teacher observed how the children responded to her work on the environment. She reflected on her own response to their response. She decided to acknowledge that they seemed pleased with the way things looked now, and she asked them for their help keeping it that way. Students were distracted from their bickering and said they would help. From that small interaction, the teacher got the idea to hold more short meetings with her students to check up on how they were doing. Was the glue getting back where it belonged, and could the books in the class library be found easily? Was their work getting into the proper bin so the aide could correct it and get it back to them? Class meetings became a time to "check in." How were they doing as a community? How were they helping each other? Were there antagonisms between kids on the playground that weren't being settled and were being brought into the room? The students, together with their teacher, forged a different kind of classroom. Instead of yelling, bribing, or threatening them, she talked with them, and they talked with each other. Over time, when I went to visit, I heard things like, "Your writing is really good!" "Your characters are always so funny," and "Thank you for helping me with that problem—you are so good at math and I just can't get it." The students started to acknowledge each other's strengths instead of competing for the teacher's attention. And the teacher? Well, the teacher went home in the evening to think about each of her students, how Carla had started to be friends with Maria, how Anthony had started to understand how to join a group, how Molly and Catrina weren't so off by themselves anymore. She could think about the lessons she would give, what sort of ties she could make to their interests, and how she could tap into their positive energy toward learning.

The teacher in this story is any educator who takes up the opportunities to participate, observe, and reflect and who then, based on the meaning made during reflection and the possibilities for action that address the situation, decides what action best serves to change the situation. In this vignette, the teacher had little energy for any type of change. Deciding on a physical change to the environment with a limited time set for it gave her the motivation to make the change. By being present to the positive response of the students, observing how she felt and how they seemed to feel, and acknowledging it, this teacher opened the door to transforming her classroom from what it had been to what it could be. She broke the cycle of negativity and built on the students' interests and their newfound strengths of "helping" from that point forward.

Transformation takes place in the teacher, in the class community, and within individual students. It takes place in "real time," which means that you are conscious of change while it is happening. Often, when we are conscious of change while it is in our midst, we can move from changing by default to, instead, changing by our choices. In the moment the teacher in our story acknowledged her own feelings in response to the children's feelings, transformation occurred. To the extent that certain changes are under our control, being conscious in real time means that we can plan or choose the changes we want. When we are conscious of change while we are in it, the likelihood of actually developing and facilitating our own and students' resilience is dramatically increased.

A Transformation Exercise

We want to close this chapter with an exercise demonstrating transformation. We invite your participation in this experiential exercise. Your reading of or participation in this exercise is completely voluntary. If you do not wish to do the exercise, please go to the next section of this chapter.

The exercise is called "Triangulation." First, take a minute to write a description of an event in your classroom. Use descriptive language. Try not to be judgmental, but note when you are. When you have described the event to your satisfaction, put it away. Now, ask two other people, perhaps one of your students, a volunteer, your aide, or someone else who participated in the event, to describe in writing that same event from their point of view. Collect the two stories. Find some uninterrupted time, maybe 15 minutes' worth, to read each of the descriptions, including yours. Note the similarities and differences among the three interpretations of that event. Note what surprises you. Note what you learn about the other two people's interests and strengths, about what they pay attention to. Note your own feelings in response to what they write.

Now that you are more aware of other people's interpretations of this event, are there any changes that you want to make? If so, what are they? Does this demand some fine-tuning in how you work? Or are their interpretations so distinct that fundamental change is called for? Understanding these differences allows for a transformation. What changes you make now are up to you.

9

Bringing It All Together

IN THE FIRST PART OF THIS BOOK we reviewed the context of resilience research and the research itself. It was found that the risk orientation, equated with a deficit view of young people, did not meet scientific rigor or today's educational needs. If educators are to help all children and youth become successful learners and make healthy decisions, then the focus of our efforts must go beyond averting potential problems. To thrive in a global economy and live compassionately in a diverse world, young people must acquire basic knowledge and skills and develop a lifelong learning process that responds to today's fast-paced, changing world.

The discovery and development of resilience is one of the most important social science advances of the 20th century. Resilience offers the possibilities of a fundamental shift in how we view and work with young people. Emerging from a serendipitous finding of people called "invulnerables," resilience evolved into a much deeper concept. Long-term studies have shown that nearly all people have strengths that can be emphasized for lifelong thriving. Thriving develops through building on the strengths of each person in the context of a supportive climate where interests and connectedness are developed. Resilience is a general approach toward young people, where individual and community support leads to a lifetime of healthy development.

In addition to the resilience research itself, there are a number of research areas supporting the direct application of resilience to education. Developmental psychology tells us that, if given proper information, young people can make coherent decisions. Physiological and educational psychology tell us that feelings directly and indirectly influence learning. From educational psychology we find that intrinsically motivated learning is more meaningful and more deeply connected to the life of the learner than extrinsically motivated learning. Social psychology research tells us that a healthy, democratic learning community produces tangible educational gains. Each of these research areas provides direct evidence for this conclusion: We can facilitate the development of thriving young people by emphasizing resilience in the educational process.

Surprisingly, the resilience approach, as has been conceived of here, has rarely been applied to education. Based on experience and research, we defined *resilience education* as "the development of decision-making and affective skills within each person and connectedness between people in the context of a healthy, democratic learning community." Based on research, practice, and our definition, some principles of practice guided the development of our approach to resilience education:

- Use strategies that engage students' intrinsic motivations.
- Allow young people to safely experiment with making decisions.
- Help create life goals, a "dream" that the learner endorses.
- Encourage the exploration of emotions related to the adversity young people face.

Please remember that in our general concept of resilience education we are not identifying which people are resilient, but rather, what resilience exists in each person.

In the second part of the book, we used these principles to develop a PORT-able approach to resilience education. Please see Figure 9.1.

Figure 9.1 represents an overview of resilience education, where you can work with those in your classroom, in your school, or in any learning context. The elements of the PORT-able model are defined as follows: *Participation* is authentic active engagement with knowledge, content, students, and learning processes that is focused in the present moment. *Observation* is noting your experiences. *Reflection* is interpreting your experiences. *Transformation* is awareness of and responsibility for an act, process, or instance of change.

The PORT-able approach is an open model, in which we facilitate change and respond to changing environments—changes in other people and changes in ourselves. We evolve in our thinking and practice by doing several things: We participate with an authentic present focus. We observe

Figure 9.1. Using a PORT-able model in resilience education.

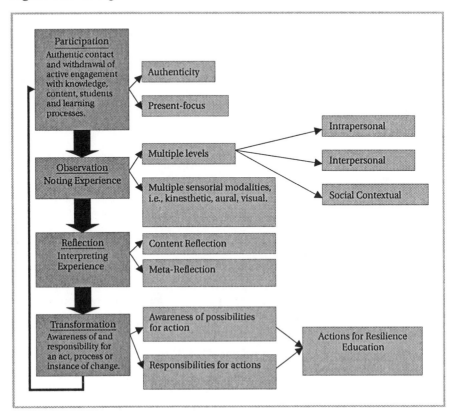

without judgment on multiple levels through multiple sensorial modalities. Observation evolves into reflection about what things mean. We interpret meaning on two levels, the content level and the metalevel. Based on different interpretations of meaning, new choices unfold before us. The availability of choices, where previously actions were taken by default, is the transformation in our understanding of what to do to facilitate resilience. Although the order in which you use the PORT-able model may vary, transformation into action will tend to follow the preceding elements. In sum, the PORT-able model can be seen as a dynamic process for facilitating and developing your own and your students' resilience.

META-REFLECTIONS ON WRITING THIS BOOK

The preceding section is a summary of what we have presented to you in this book. Below are some observations and reflections on what we have learned in the process of writing this book.

Thriving Based on Our Connectedness With You

This was a challenging book to write. Although we may never know the majority of readers who have decided to pick this book up, we have been enriched by the endeavor. This is not a cavalier point. Part of what keeps us going is the opportunity to use our own creativity to develop a book on a topic of our interest in a way that might interest you. We were emotionally connected, if only in perception, with you, the reader. So we perceived some level of mutuality, and this drove us toward completion. Our perception of mutuality or connectedness with you spurred us on to further develop our writing strengths and our interest in creativity by challenging ourselves to develop an experiential literary format.

The perception of emotional connectedness, strength, and interest development leads us to another conclusion. It is precisely these factors that keep us from burning out on writing, talking, and practicing resilience after so many years. As we perceive a connectedness with you, our readers, and the possibility that these ideas will make a difference for you and your students, we feel that we too are growing and learning.

Health of the Helper

As we meta-reflect, another related issue comes into our consciousness. We have an appreciation and a concern. We appreciate the work educators are doing to develop and deliver resilience education. The mutual rewards that both educator and students experience from resilience education are great. However, we are concerned about the health of the helper. To this point we have not discussed the political realities that many educators face every day. The current context we are operating in is best described by one word, *Standardistas*, which comes from the excellent book by Susan O'Hanian (1999) *One Size Fits Few: The Folly of Educational Standards*. The title alone makes it clear that she challenges the notion that educational standards are an effective way of educating young people. She identifies the people who believe in using such standards as "Standardistas." Whether we like it or not, standards-driven education is *the* current educational context. We do not want to tell you, the educator, to go in and blindly implement resilience education. This may be hazardous to your professional health. Indeed, the health of the helper is of utmost importance to us. We want to say more about this.

There are responses to the contexts that the Standardistas represent. By picking up this book, you are at least interested in an alternative way of viewing the educational process. To the extent that you determine it is a potentially valuable tool for working with your students, resilience education now becomes a matter of professional development. Professional development is taking into account the latest that is available in your field, applying it in your practice, and sharing it with those with whom you work. In a positive sense, resilience education becomes your responsibility. Taking responsibility for our own development and being agents of change can be challenging, but under the right conditions taking responsibility can be empowering.

By its very definition, the PORT-able resilience educational approach helps you become an effective agent of change. In one way, using the resilience education model in the context of your educational system is similar to working with young people. This is because built into the approach is explicit observation and reflection on the current educational system. Your actions to create change in your school or district are guided by your observations and reflections on those observations, followed by conscious decisions about which actions might produce the best results. This allows you to create change by choice rather than by default. The model allows you to promote systemic change in ways that you believe will maintain your health while maintaining an orientation toward change. Resilience education provides you with the means to appreciate and respond to the political wind that the Standardistas represent while continuing to thrive in your professional practice.

The Elephant in the Room

When we look across this book, we want to acknowledge the elephant in the room—evaluation. We believe that there has been some significant evaluation of aspects of resilience education. We look forward to and support further evaluation of this model in its totality. However, if resilience education is as different as we believe it to be, we need to use an evaluation model that accurately represents the experiences of educators, young people, and others who are participating in resilience education. We will not go into the details of what such an evaluation model might look like. That is for another book. Suffice to say that in the past these models have not been developed, and it is likely that many potentially positive effects have been missed. For further information about the challenges of the past and an alternative model, please see Horowitz and Brown (1996). In sum of this point, the only way that we can capture the effects of the PORT-able model of resilience is to shift how and what we evaluate, from focusing on narrow aspects of learning toward evaluating learning and development.

CLOSING META-REFLECTIONS

Today, the world is getting smaller. People are closer both virtually (i.e., through the World Wide Web and the media) and actually (i.e., through global transportation). By our very proximity, the nature of our well-being becomes increasingly interdependent. An educational system that does not allow us to engage one another, with all the changes that come about as a result of our evolving closeness, does not address what it means to learn or to thrive. This is a global concept with personal implications. To effectively participate today, young people need to make connections with others as well as to step back. They need to make connections with others so that they feel like they belong. They need to develop their sense of self so that their imaginations can soar. By connecting with others and furthering their own development intellectually, emotionally, and spiritually, they can then lead us to possibilities that we cannot even imagine right now.

Resilience education is not about nice touchy-feely platitudes. It is a specific and dynamic learning and developmental process. It allows young people to unleash the power that each intrinsically has. This is the power to learn and acquire a lifelong learning process. This is the power to connect with and to realistically chart their own destinies. It is not just for the young people who exist under the worst of life's conditions. Resilience education allows us to facilitate the development of all young people.

The most wonderful parallel of the resilience education process is that each of the powers that are developed in service of the student are the same powers available to the professional educator who uses resilience education.

In this book we shared an adventure of a particular kind. You were able to choose your own adventure. You were able to choose which parts of the book you wanted to explore or which exercises you wanted to do. Making choices represents a step in resilience education. We hope that by making your choices explicit and combining them with a highly relevant subject, resilience education was initiated in you. Making choices is not the only strategy we have used. It is simply a step that we wanted to acknowledge because it provided you with possibilities for deeper engagement in this book.

Once again, "The Opportunities" are knocking. If anything, this book has provided you with a choice. Won't you close the parable by taking the chance to develop your own and your students' interests, strengths, and connectedness? We close extending our appreciation to you for reading our book.

References

Anthony, E. J., & Cohler, B. J. (Eds.). (1987). *The invulnerable child.* New York: Guilford.

Baizerman, M., & Compton, D. (1992). From respondent and informant to consultant and participant: The evolution of a state agency policy evaluation. In A. M. Madison (Ed.), *Minority issues in program evaluation* (New Directions in Program Evaluation, Vol. 53, pp. 5-16). San Francisco: Jossey-Bass.

Barott, J. E., & Kleiveland, J. (1996). The confluent approach to organizational change and development. In J. H. Brown (Ed.), *Advances in confluent education: Integrating consciousness for human change: Vol. 1* (pp. 63-80). Greenwich, CT: JAI.

Baumrind, D., & Moselle, K. A. (1985). A developmental perspective on adolescent drug abuse. *Advances in Alcohol and Substance Abuse, 4*(3/4), 41-67.

Bell, N. J., & Bell, R. W. (1993). *Adolescent risk taking.* Newbury Park, CA: Sage.

Benard, B. (1987). *Protective factor research: What we can learn from resilient children* (Report for Prevention Resource Center, Western Center for Prevention). Portland, OR: Western Center for Prevention.

Benard, B. (1994). The health realization approach to resiliency. *Western Center News, 8*(1), 1-4.

Benard, B. (1996). Creating resiliency-enhancing schools: Relationships, motivating beliefs, and schoolwide reform. *Resiliency in Action, 1*(2), 5-8.

Benard, B. (1999). Mentoring: New study shows the power of relationship to make a difference. In N. Henderson, B. Benard, & N. Sharp-Light (Eds.), *Resiliency in action: Practical ideas for overcoming risks and building strengths in youth, families and communities* (pp. 93-99). Gorham, ME: Resiliency in Action.

Benson, P. (1998). *All kids are our kids.* San Francisco: Jossey-Bass.

Blue-Swadener, B., & Lubeck, S. (1995). *Children and families "at promise": Deconstructing the discourse of risk.* Albany: State University of New York Press.

Bredekamp, S. (1986). *Developmentally appropriate practice in early childhood programs serving children from birth to age 8.* Washington, DC: National Association for the Education of Young Children.

Brofenbrenner, U. (1979). *The ecology of human development.* Cambridge, MA: Harvard University Press.

Brown, G. I. (1969). Awareness training and creativity based on gestalt therapy. *Journal of Contemporary Psychotherapy, 2,* 25-32.

Brown, G. I. (1990). *Human teaching for human learning: An introduction to confluent learning.* Highland, NY: Gestalt Journal. (Original work published 1972)

Brown, G. I. (1975). *The live classroom: Innovation through confluent education and gestalt.* New York: Viking.

Brown, J. H. (Ed.). (1996). *Advances in confluent education: Integrating consciousness for human change: Vol. 1.* Greenwich, CT: JAI.

Brown, J. H. (1999). The multicultural dynamics of educational change. In Z. Cline, J. Necochea, & J. H. Brown (Eds.), *Advances in confluent education: Vol. 2. Multicultural dynamics of educational change* (pp. 169-189). Greenwich, CT: JAI.

Brown, J. H., & D'Emidio-Caston, M. (1995). On becoming at risk through drug education: How symbolic policies and their practices affect students. *Evaluation Review, 19,* 451-492.

Brown, J. H., & Horowitz, J. E. (1993). Deviance and deviants: Why adolescent substance use prevention programs do not work. *Evaluation Review, 17,* 529-555.

Brown, J. R. (1996). *The I in science: Training to utilize subjectivity in research.* Boston: Scandinavian University Press.

California State Department of Education. (1991-1992). *Healthy kids, healthy California drug, alcohol, tobacco, education (DATE) district application for funding.* Sacramento, CA: Author.

Camus, A. (1942). *The stranger.* New York: Vintage.

Cline, Z., Necochea, J., & Brown, J. H. (Eds.). (1999). *Advances in confluent education: Vol. 2. Multicultural dynamics of educational change.* Greenwich, CT: JAI.

Coalition for Essential Schools. (1999). *Principles at work II: Measuring the success of the Coalition of Essential Schools: A 1999-2000 report from the CES network.* Oakland, CA: Author.

Coie, J. D., Watt, N. F., West, S. G., Hawkins, J. D., Asarnow, J. R., Markman, H. J., Ramey, S. L., Shure, M. B., & Long, B. (1993). The science of prevention: A conceptual framework and some directions for a national research program. *American Psychologist, 48,* 1013-1022.

D'Arcangelo, M. (1998, November). The brains behind the brain. *Educational Leadership* [On-line serial], *56*(3).
Available: http://www.ascd. org/pubs/el/nov98/exttoc.html

Darling-Hammond, L. (1997). *The right to learn.* San Francisco: Jossey-Bass.

Deci, E. L., & Ryan, R. M. (1985). *Intrinsic motivation and self determination in human behavior.* New York: Plenum.

Dewey, J. (1897). My pedagogic creed. *School Journal, 54*(3), 77-80.

Dewey, J. (1899). *The school and society.* Chicago: University of Chicago Press.

Dewey, J. (1902). *The child and the curriculum.* Chicago: University of Chicago Press.

Dryfoos, J. (1994). *Full-service schools: A revolution in health and social services for children, youth, and families.* San Francisco: Jossey-Bass.

Dryfoos, J. (1998). *Safe passage: Making it through adolescence in a risky society.* New York: Oxford University Press.

Eccles, J. S., & Midgley, C. (1989). Stage/environment fit: Developmentally appropriate classrooms for early adolescents. In R. E. Ames & C. Ames (Eds.), *Research on motivation in education: Vol. 3* (pp. 139-186). San Diego, CA: Academic Press.

Eccles, J. S., Midgley, C., & Adler, T. (1984). Grade related changes in the school environment: Effects of achievement motivation. In J. G. Nicholls (Ed.), *The development of achievement motivation* (pp. 283-331). Greenwich, CT: JAI.

Eccles, J. S., Midgley, C., Wigfield, A., Miller-Buchanan, C. M., Reuman, D., Flanagan, C., & McIver, D. (1993). Development during adolescence: The impact of stage-environment fit on young adolescents' experiences in schools and in families. *American Psychologist, 48,* 90-101.

Edelman, M. (1964). *The symbolic uses of politics.* Chicago: University of Chicago Press.

Fine, M. (1993). Making controversy: Who's "at risk"? In R. Wollons (Ed.), *Children at risk in America* (pp. 91-110). Albany: State University of New York Press.

Fischhoff, B. (1975). Hindsight does not equal foresight: The effect of outcome knowledge on judgement under uncertainty. *Journal of Experimental Psychology: Human Perception and Performance, 104,* 288-299.

Fischhoff, B. (1989). Making decisions about AIDS. In V. Mays, G. Albee, & S. Schneider (Eds.), *Primary prevention of AIDS* (pp. 168-205). Newbury Park, CA: Sage.

Forgione, P. D. (1998). *Statement of Pascal D. Forgione, Jr., Ph.D., U.S. Commissioner of Education Statistics, National Center for Education Statistics (NCES) on the release of U.S. report on Grade 12 results from the Third International Mathematics and Science Study (TIMSS), February 24, 1998* [On-line]. Available: www.nces.ed.gov/Pressrelease/timssrelease.html

Gardner, H. (1993). *Frames of mind: The theory of multiple intelligences.* New York: Basic Books.

Gardner, H. (1999). *Intelligence reframed: Multiple intelligences for the 21st century.* New York: Basic Books.

Garmezy, N. (1983). Stressors of childhood. In N. Garmezy & M. Rutter (Eds.), *Stress, coping and development in children* (pp. 43-84). New York: McGraw-Hill.

Garmezy, N. (1987). Stress, competence, and development: Continuities in the study of schizophrenic adults, children vulnerable to psychopathology, and the search for stress-resistant children. *American Journal of Orthopsychiatry, 52,* 159-175.

Garmezy, N. (1991). Resilience and vulnerability to adverse developmental outcomes associated with poverty. *American Behavioral Scientist, 34,* 416-430.

Gillmore, M. R., Hawkins, D. J., Catalano, R. F., Day, L. E., Moore, M., & Abbott, R. (1991). Structure of problem behaviors in preadolescence. *Journal of Consulting and Clinical Psychology, 59,* 499-506.

Goleman, D. (1996). *Emotional intelligence: Why it can matter more than I.Q.* New York: Bantam.

Goleman, D. (1998). *Working within emotional intelligence.* New York: Bantam.

Hawkins, J. D., Catalano, R. F., & Miller, J. Y. (1992). Risk and protective factors for alcohol and other drug problems in adolescence and early adulthood: Implications for substance abuse prevention. *Psychological Bulletin, 112,* 63-105.

Hawkins, J. D., Lishner, D. M., Jenson, J. M., & Catalano, R. F. (1987). Delinquents and drugs: What the evidence suggests about prevention and treatment programming. In B. S. Brown & A. R. Mills (Eds.), *Youth at high risk for substance abuse* (DHHS Publication No. ADM 87-1537, pp. 81-131). Washington, DC: U.S. Government Printing Office.

Heider, G. (1966). Vulnerability in infants and young children: A pilot study. *Genetic Psychology Monographs, 73*(1), 1-216.

Hinkle, L. E. (1974). The effect of exposure to culture change, social change, and changes in interpersonal relationships on health. In B. S. Dohrenwend & B. P. Dohrenwend (Eds.), *Stressful life events.* New York: John Wiley.

Horowitz, J. E., & Brown, J. H. (1996). Confluent education and evaluation research. In J. H. Brown (Ed.), *Advances in confluent education: Integrating consciousness for human change: Vol. 1* (pp. 113-141). Greenwich, CT: JAI.

Jessor, R. (1976). Predicting time of onset of marijuana use: A developmental study of high school youth. *Journal of Consulting and Clinical Psychology, 44,* 125-134.

Jessor, R. (1992). Risk behavior in adolescence: A psychosocial framework for understanding and action. In D. E. Rogers & E. Ginzburg (Eds.), *Adolescents at risk: Medical and social perspectives* (pp. 19-34). Boulder, CO: Westview.

Jessor, R. (1993). Successful adolescent development among youth in high risk settings. *American Psychologist, 48,* 117-126.

Jessor, R., & Jessor, S. L. (1977). *Problem behavior and psychosocial development: A longitudinal study of youth.* New York: Academic Press.

Johnston, L. D., O'Malley, P. M., & Bachman, J. G. (1999). *National survey results on drug use from the Monitoring the Future Survey Study (1975-1998).* Rockville, MD: National Institute on Drug Abuse.

Kohlberg, R., & Meyer, R. (1972). Development as the aim of education. *Harvard Educational Review, 42,* 449-496.

Kohn, A. (1996). *Beyond discipline: From compliance to community.* Alexandria, VA: Association for Supervision and Curriculum Development.

Kumpfer, K. (1990). Environmental and family-focused prevention: The Cinderellas of prevention want to go to the ball, too. In K. H. Rey, C. Faegre, & P. Lowery (Eds.), *Prevention research findings: 1988* (OSAP Prevention Monograph No. 3, DHHS Publication No. ADM 89-1615, pp. 194-220). Washington, DC: U.S. Government Printing Office.

Lewin, K. (1935). *A dynamic theory of personality.* New York: McGraw-Hill.

Liotts, R. F., Jason, L. A., & DuPont, P. J. (1983). The relevance of developmental theory for preventive drug education programs. *Bulletin of the Society of Psychologists of Addictive Behaviors,* 2179-2188.

Modzeleski, W. J. (1995). *Research and funding announcement from W. J. Modzeleski, Director, Safe and Drug Free Schools Program, June 14, 1995.*

Washington, DC: U.S. Department of Education: Office of Elementary and Secondary Education.

Montessori, M. (1912). *The Montessori method.* New York: Frederick Stokes.

Morgan, G. (1986). *Images of organization.* Beverly Hills, CA: Sage.

Moriarty, A. E. (1961). Coping patterns of preschool children in response to intelligence test demands. *Genetic Psychology Monographs, 64,* 3-127.

Moriarty, A. E. (1987). Further reflections on resilience. In E. J. Anthony & B. J. Cohler (Eds.), *The invulnerable child* (pp. 78-91). New York: Guilford.

Murphy, L. B. (1956). *Personality and young children: Vol. 2. Colin, a normal child.* New York: Basic Books.

Murphy, L. B. (1962). *The widening world of childhood.* New York: Basic Books.

Murphy, L. B., & Moriarty, A. E. (1976). *Vulnerability, coping and growth.* New Haven, CT: Yale University Press.

Newcomb, M., & Bentler, P. (1988). *Consequences of adolescent drug use: Impact on the lives of young adults.* Newbury Park, CA: Sage.

Noddings, N. (1992). *The challenge to schools.* New York: Teachers College Press.

O'Connell Higgins, G. (1994). *Resilient adults: Overcoming a cruel past.* New York: Simon & Schuster.

Office of Substance Abuse Prevention. (1989). *Request for proposals for high-risk youth grants.* Washington, DC: U.S. Office of Substance Abuse Prevention.

O'Hanian, S. (1999). *One size fits few: The folly of educational standards.* New York: Heinemann.

Perls, F. (1973). *The gestalt approach and eye witness to therapy.* Palo Alto, CA: Science and Behavior Books.

Perls, F. (1988). *Gestalt therapy verbatim.* Highland, NY: Gestalt Journal.

Piaget, J. (1929). *The child's conception of the world.* London: Routledge & Kegan Paul.

Piaget, J. (1973). *To understand is to invent.* New York: Grossman.

Placier, M. L. (1993). The semantics of state policy making: The case of "at-risk." *Educational Evaluation and Policy Analysis, 15,* 380-395.

Quandrel, M. J. (1990). *Elicitation of adolescents' risk perceptions: Qualitative and quantitative dimensions.* Unpublished doctoral dissertation, Carnegie Mellon University, Pittsburgh, PA.

Quandrel, M. J., Fischhoff, B., & Davis, W. (1993). Adolescent (in)vulnerability. *American Psychologist, 48,* 102-116.

Resnick, M. D., Bearman, P. S., Blum, R. W., Bauman, K. E., Harris, K. M., Jones, J., Tabor, J., Beunring, T., Sieving, R. E., Shew, M., Ireland, M., Bearinger, L. H., & Udry, J. R. (1997). Protecting adolescents from harm. *Journal of the American Medical Association, 278,* 823-832.

Richardson, G., & Gray, D. (1999). Resilient youth: A resiliency-fostering curriculum for secondary schools. In N. Henderson, B. Benard, & N. Sharp-Light (Eds.), *Resiliency in action: Practical ideas for overcoming risks and building strengths in youth, families and communities* (pp. 31-38). Gorham, ME: Resiliency in Action.

Richardson, V. (1990). At-risk programs: Evaluation and critical inquiry. *New Directions for Program Evaluation, 45,* 61-75.

Rossi, R. J. (Ed.). (1994). *Schools and students at risk: Context and framework for positive change.* New York: Teachers College Press.

Rutter, M. (1979). Protective factors in children's responses to stress and disadvantage. In M. W. Ken & J. E. Rolf (Eds.), *Primary prevention of psychopathology: Vol. 3. Social competence in children* (pp. 324-338). Hanover, NH: University Press of New England.

Rutter, M. (1981). Stress, coping and development: Some issues and some questions. *Journal of Child Psychology and Psychiatry, 22,* 323-356.

Rutter, M. (1985). Resilience in the face of adversity: Protective factors and resistance to psychiatric disorder. *British Journal of Psychiatry, 147,* 598-611.

Rutter, M. (1987). Psychosocial resilience and protective mechanisms. *American Journal of Orthopsychiatry, 57,* 316-331.

Rutter, M. (1991). Childhood experiences and adult psychosocial functioning. *Ciba Foundation Symposium,* 189-200; discussion, 200-208.

Steiner, R. (1988). *The child's changing consciousness and Waldorf education.* London: Steiner Press.

Sylwester, R. (1995). *A celebration of neurons: An educator's guide to the human brain.* Alexandria, VA: Association for Supervision and Curriculum Development.

Takanishi, R. (1993). The opportunities of adolescence—Research, interventions, and policy: Introduction to the special issue. *American Psychologist, 48,* 85-87.

Thayer-Bacon, B., & Bacon, C. (1997). *Philosophy applied to education: Nurturing a democratic community in the classroom.* Englewood Cliffs, NJ: Prentice Hall.

Tierney, J. P., Baldwin-Grossman, J., & Resch, N. L. (1995). *Making a difference: An impact study of Big Brothers/Big Sisters.* Philadelphia: Public/Private Ventures.

Von Schlippe, G. (1993). "Guilty!" Thoughts in relation to my own past: Letters to my son. In B. Heimannsberg & C. J. Schmidt (Eds.), *The collective silence: German identity and the legacy of shame* (p. 210). San Francisco: Jossey-Bass.

Watson, M., Battistich, V., & Solomon, D. (1997). Enhancing students' social and ethical development in schools: An intervention program and its effects. *International Journal of Educational Research, 27*, 571-586.

Wátzlawick, P., Weakland, J. H., & Fisch, R. (1974). *Change: Principles of problem formation and problem resolution.* New York: Norton.

Werner, E. E. (1986). Resilient offspring of alcoholics: A longitudinal study from birth to age 18. *Journal of Studies on Alcohol, 47*(1), 34-40.

Werner, E. E. (1989). High risk children in young adulthood: A longitudinal study from birth to 32 years. *American Journal of Orthopsychiatry, 59*, 72-81.

Werner, E. E. (1993). Risk, resilience and recovery: Perspectives from the Kauai Longitudinal Study. *Development and Psychopathology, 5*, 503-515.

Werner, E. E., Bierman, J., & French, F. (1971). *The children of Kauai.* Honolulu: University of Hawaii Press.

Werner, E. E., & Smith, R. S. (1977). *Kauai's children come of age.* Honolulu: University of Hawaii Press.

Werner, E. E., & Smith, R. S. (1982). *Vulnerable but invincible: A longitudinal study of resilient children and youth.* New York: McGraw-Hill.

Index

CORWIN
PRESS

The Corwin Press logo—a raven striding across an open book—represents the happy union of courage and learning. We are a professional-level publisher of books and journals for K–12 educators, and we are committed to creating and providing resources that embody these qualities. Corwin's motto is "Success for All Learners."